The Pocket Guide to

DICE &
DICE GAMES

For Aidan, a fellow dice and conjuring enthusiast.
Iacta alea est

The Pocket Guide to

DICE &
DICE GAMES

Dr. Keith Souter

Illustrations by Laura Matine

SKYHORSE PUBLISHING

Copyright © 2012, 2013 by Keith Souter

First published in Great Britain in 2012 by Remember When, an imprint of Pen & Sword Books Ltd.

All Rights Reserved. No part of this book may be reproduced in any manner without the express written consent of the publisher, except in the case of brief excerpts in critical reviews or articles. All inquiries should be addressed to Skyhorse Publishing, 307 West 36th Street, 11th Floor, New York, NY 10018.

Skyhorse Publishing books may be purchased in bulk at special discounts for sales promotion, corporate gifts, fund-raising, or educational purposes. Special editions can also be created to specifications. For details, contact the Special Sales Department, Skyhorse Publishing, 307 West 36th Street, 11th Floor, New York, NY 10018 or info@skyhorsepublishing.com.

Skyhorse® and Skyhorse Publishing® are registered trademarks of Skyhorse Publishing, Inc.®, a Delaware corporation.

Visit our website at www.skyhorsepublishing.com.

10 9 8 7 6 5 4 3 2

Library of Congress Cataloging-in-Publication Data is available on file.

ISBN: 978-1-62087-180-5

Printed in China

Contents

Acknowledgements

There are several people that I would like to thank for helping me with this book on dice and dice games. Firstly, I would like to thank Laura Matine, my talented illustrator who has been a pleasure to work with. She deftly turned my ideas, crude sketches and the odd video clip into first rate pieces of artwork.

Fiona Shoop was the commissioning editor at Pen & Sword who actually came up with the original idea for the book and I am grateful to her for the work that we did on it in those early days.

Lisa Hooson has been extremely helpful in taking the book from manuscript to finished work. Thank you, Lisa.

The cover really sets the book off and I have to thank David Hemingway for coming up with the idea of the 5s dice.

Dr. Irving Finkel kindly allowed me to include images of the game of Senet and the Royal Game of Ur, which Laura Matine so skilfully reproduced. I thank him for this. Fishbourne Roman Palace allowed me to include the photograph of Roman dice which had been discovered in excavation of the site. I am grateful to them.

A really big thank you to my wonderful agent Isabel Atherton at Creative Authors who set the dice rolling with this one.

Thank you to Joe Sverchek, my editor at Skyhorse, who has been a delight to work with.

And finally, thanks to my wife Rachel for putting up with the incessant clatter of dice as I practiced and experimented for this book.

The dice of Zeus fall ever luckily

Sophocles (497–405 BC)

A Personal Note

My interest in magic began with a die.

That's right, I said with a 'die'. A lot of people are not aware that the correct term for a numbered cube is 'die'. The word 'dice' is the plural. The word comes from the old French dé, itself derived from the Latin datum, meaning 'the given thing'.

Anyway, back to the die that sparked my interest. It was a trick die that was part of a conjuring set I had been given for my sixth birthday. The trick was called The Dissolving Die. The die in question was made of wood and was about two inches square with a hole bored through it. The conjurer (that was me) showed the audience two ropes that had been passed through the hole.

A simple knot was tied with the top rope ensnaring the die securely.

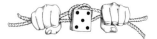

Then as I lifted the die by the securing ropes I cried out the magic word ABRACADABRA and suddenly the die just melted through the two ropes, which were then available for anyone to examine.

It was a simple trick but the audience reaction never failed. I was hooked on conjuring from that moment and ever since then dice have been objects of fascination and potential mystery for me. In this book I hope to show you just how fascinating they can be.

Part 1

The Many Uses of Dice Through the Ages

Chapter 1

Roʟʟ the Dice – The Early Games

Iacta alea est – The die is cast

Julius Caesar crossing the Rubicon

It is unclear where dice were first used. We tend to associate them in modern times with games and gaming, yet it is highly likely that they were originally used as divinatory aids in the hands of early medicine men or women. The way that they fell would be considered under the control of a deity and the shaman, as the interpreter of the deity's answers, would be thought to have a direct line to the divine.

Almost inevitably, games would have developed using early dice, so one can think of them as the ancient world's leisure equivalent of the television.

From the mists of time

A tablet found in the Great Pyramid of Giza, dated to about 3000 BC, describes a game of dice played by the gods in order to add five days to the calendar. It was said that Ra, the god of all creation had decreed that Nut, the sky goddess could not produce a child on any day of the calendar, which at that time had 360 days. Thoth, the god of the night and of arithmetic, writing and medicine, usually depicted as a man with an ibis head, or as a dog-headed baboon, interceded on her behalf by playing dice with the moon. He won five days of the moon's light, allowing Nut to give birth and the calendar was increased to 365 days.

Greek myth also tells of their gods dicing with a knucklebone for control of the different kingdoms. Zeus won the heavens, Poseidon won the seas and Hades won the underworld.

Sophocles (496–406 BC), the great Greek tragedian, claimed that dice had been invented to entertain and amuse the troops by Palomedes during the siege of Troy, the city at the heart of the Trojan War in about 1000 BC.

The Greek historian Herodotus of Halicarnassus (485–425 BC), wrote in his great work *History*, that the Lydians of Asia Minor actually invented dice as a diversion from famine during the days of King Atys.

Plutarch (46–120 AD), a later Greek historian and biographer, writes in his *Life of Artarxerxes* about a dice game played between King Artarxerxes II of Persia and his mother, Parysatis. Although Artarxerxes was her eldest son, her favourite had been Cyrus, who (according to Plutarch) had been murdered and decapitated by Tissaphernes, upon the orders of Artarxerxes. Patysatis deliberately let Artarxerxes win at first, gradually increasing the stakes, until the stakes included Tissaphernes. Parysatis then won and in revenge for the murder of her favourite son had him flailed and executed.

The Bible tells of Roman centurions playing dice for Christ's clothing at the crucifixion.

The ancient Indian text the Mahabharata describes how Yudhisthira, the son of King Pandu, played dice against the Kauravas, the sons of King Kuru, for the kingdom of Hastinapura; the result being a great war.

All of these references are pure speculation or come from the myths of various cultures, yet they indicate that dice had a great value for distraction and for gambling, even among the gods – sometimes with awesome consequences.

Persia and the Serpent Board Game

Archaeology has given us actual evidence of the use of dice from ancient times. In 2004 news of a board game containing dice was excavated at Shahr-i Sokhta, the legendary Burnt City, an ancient Persian site in modern day Iran. This has been carbon-dated as being 5,000 years old, but it is thought to have been imported from India.

The board was made from ebony and had an engraved snake coiling around itself 20 times to produce 20 slots for laying playing pieces.

Figure 1: The Serpent Board Game.

Mesopotamia and the Royal Game of Ur

In the 1920s Sir Leonard Woolley was excavating in the ancient city of Ur in Mesopotamia, or modern day Iraq. While excavating the royal tombs in the city he discovered two game boards dating back to the first dynasty, or about 2500 BC. Accordingly, archaeologists called it the Royal Game of Ur or the Game of Twenty Squares. One of the boards is now on show at the British Museum.

The game was played by two players on a grid of 20 squares, arranged as a set of 12 squares and another set of six squares linked by a bridge of two squares as in Figure 2. As you can see, it is not dissimilar to the Serpent game from Shahr-i Sokhta.

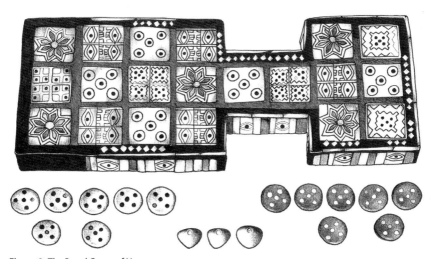

Figure 2: The Royal Game of Ur.

There was speculation about the rules for many years until 2007 when Dr. Irving Finkel, an Assyriologist at the British Museum and the world's foremost authority on ancient board games, deciphered a cuneiform tablet that had been written by the Babylonian scribe Itti-Marduk-balatu in 177 BC. This clay tablet had been stored in the British Museum since the end of the nineteenth century. Using this and photographs of another ancient tablet that had been destroyed during the First World War, Dr Finkel was able to work out the exact rules of the game. Itti-Marduk-balatu had effectively written a treatise about the national game of ancient Babylon.

It was both a race game and a betting game. It was played with two sets of five or seven markers; one set of white and one of black. Either four-sided stick dice or tetrahedral (four-sided) dice with marked corners were used. Throws of one through four were all that was needed to play. The grid has five squares with rosettes, five with eyes and five with circled dots. The remaining five have a variety of dots.

Players had to throw to get their pieces on the board and had to move all of the pieces from the start square to exit from the middle square at the end of the eight square grid. The rosettes were considered lucky squares and would be the only ones that could be occupied by more than one piece.

The aim was to get all of one's pieces onto the board and negotiate a way around on one of two tracks, knocking your opponent's pieces off if you could. Knocked off pieces had to begin again. The winner was the person who first got all of his pieces off the board.

As the name implies, the Royal Game of Ur was a game for the nobility. A simpler game was available or developed by the lower orders of society. This common game is thought to have been played with five pieces each and two dice.

We have evidence of this from graffiti found on various Assyrian or Mesopotamian monuments that are housed in the world's museums. A graffito grid of such a game was found etched on the foundation of one of a pair of human-headed winged bull sentinels of an Assyrian gateway from the palace of Sargon II, which is on exhibition in the British Museum. It is believed to have been made and used by sentries at the gateway in about

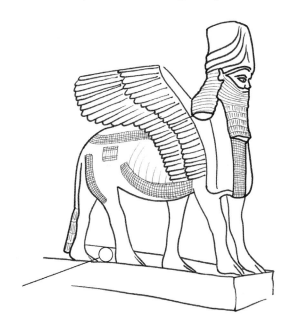

Figure 3: There is a crudely etched simple version of the Royal Game of Ur on this Assyrian gateway sentinel in the British Museum.

710 BC. Fascinatingly, similar etched grids have been found on other Assyrian monuments in the Louvre in Paris and in Nineveh in Iraq. This version was played with two dice and five game pieces each.

Egypt and Senet

As we shall see in a little more detail in the next chapter, the earliest types of dice were made from the ankle bones of hoofed animals, specifically the talus bone or astragalus. These commonly became known as 'knucklebones'. Their use seemed to spread across the ancient world and indeed, in some remote regions of Mongolia, they are still used.

Early Egyptian knucklebones were used in pre-dynastic times, or before the days of the pharaohs. Several museums around the world have examples of these, including the British Museum and the Egyptian Museum in Berlin.

Senet may well rival the Royal Game of Ur as the oldest dice and board game in the world, for it is also known to have been played over five thousand years ago in pre-dynastic times, before the invention of writing. It was played on a board of 30 squares arranged in three rows of 10. Several sets were

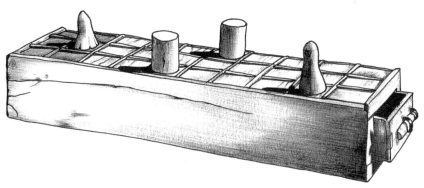

Figure 4: *The ancient Egyptian game of Senet.*

famously found in the tomb of the pharaoh Tutankhamun (c. 1371–1352 BC). Intriguingly, some of these sets have a Senet board on one side and the Royal Game of Ur on the other. That is tantalising, because it does not tell us which came first.

The British Museum also has a set of knucklebones and other throwing sticks used in the game of Senet dating from 1350 BC, which were found in the tomb of Nebamun, an accountant in the Temple of Amun at Thebes (modern day Karnack).

Although there is a hieroglyph in the shape of a Senet board in profile there are no rules of the game of Senet in existence. Nevertheless archaeologists have enough full sets available to them to speculate, probably with a fair degree of accuracy, about the way it was played. It seems to have been played with seven pieces for each of two players, who took turns in throwing sticks or knucklebones to make a move. It was a tactical race game in which one could block and possibly remove one's opponent's pieces.

The Pharoah Rameses III (1182–1151 BC) is portrayed on a gate pylon at his temple at Medinet Haboo, playing dice with two women. It is likely that he was playing a board game with them rather than a gambling game.

The Romans and Ludus Duodecim Scriptorum

Dice certainly came into their own in Roman times. The most famous and widely played board game was *Ludus Duodecim Scriptorum*, meaning the Game of Twelve Points. This game was played with a board of three rows of 12 squares, which in time was reduced to two rows. It was played with up to 15 pieces each and three actual dice. Like Senet and the Royal Game of Ur, the exact rules are not know, but it is thought to have a good claim to be the original version of backgammon.

Chapter 2

From Knucklebones to Cyber-Dice

God's dice always have a lucky roll

Sophocles (497–405 BC)

The first dice were made from the ankle bones of hoofed animals, like sheep, goats and oxen. The specific bone is the talus, otherwise known as the astragalus. It is basically tetrahedral in shape, so that it can land in one of four positions. Thus they became known by the Greeks and Romans as astralgi or knucklebones. Each face is distinguishable from the others. One face is concave, one is convex, the third is almost flat and the fourth is slightly undulating. Presumably they were used as divinatory tools to begin with, only later being used in various games, such as those we looked at in Chapter 1.

At some stage people began marking them, perhaps with mystical signs to further enhance the contact with the divine. Then when numbers became commonly used these were added.

The Greeks and Romans then started to make dice from other materials, such as wood, metal, ivory, bone and animal horn. When they adopted the cube as the standard shape it was necessary to differentiate the sides, hence they were numbered one to six. Over the years archaeologists have accumulated many examples from antiquity. In 1884 Sir Flinders Petrie, the first professor of Egyptology, discovered a limestone six-sided die, complete with bored holes to show numbers, at Naucratis, an ancient city in the Nile delta.

Roman dice have been found in many archaeological sites around the world, including Pompeii and Herculaneum, the twin towns at the tip of Italy which were fossilised in time when Mount Vesuvius erupted in 79 AD. The interesting thing is that gambling was actually illegal in

Figure 5: Playing with knucklebones.

the Roman Empire at that time except during the Saturnalia festival. This officially took place on 17 December and went on until 23 December. It was held in honour of Saturn, the god of agriculture. During this festival there was feasting, merrymaking and a relaxing of the normal laws, including that against gambling. Gifts were exchanged and even slaves were permitted rare free time.

Frescos found on the Via di Mercurio in Pompeii depict players gambling with dice. The sheer number of dice found around the town indicates that they were not merely used during Saturnalia, but were commonly played in disregard to the law. Even more interestingly, it is said that several sets of loaded dice were found. Clearly, there were not just gamblers in the Roman world; there were out and out hustlers.

Figure 6 shows fragments of Roman dice and how they would have looked, these were found during the excavation of a Roman palace at Fishbourne, in Sussex.

In early medieval times dicing was virtually driven underground by the Church, yet as with many illegal activities it thrived. By the Middle Ages dicing and all manner of dice games were being played by all levels of society. The nobility played with sophisticated game boards and ivory dice, and the less well off manufactured dice from stone, bone and wood. Guilds sprang up for dice makers and schools of dicing called *scholiae deciorum* were established to teach the various games and methods of throwing.

Figure 6: *Roman dice from the palace at Fishbourne.*

The Canterbury Tales

Geoffrey Chaucer (1343–1400), England's first great poet, penned *The Canterbury Tales* in rhyming couplets. It is an epic poem that really heralds the beginning of the English novel. It is a collection of tales recounted by individual members of a group of pilgrims as they make their way from the Tabard Inn in London's Southwark to the shrine of Saint Thomas à Becket at Canterbury Cathedral. In *The Cook's Tale* the Cook introduces the character of an apprentice to the victualler's guild who is a renowned trickster, especially with the dice.

> *For in the toune nas ther no prentys*
> *That fairer koude caste a paire of dys*

And in *The Pardoner's Tale*, he tells of three young men who spend every night in various taverns drinking and playing dice. It is likely that they played a game known as 'hazard'. It was, as the name implied, a game that could be dangerous to the unwary, for there were men such as these who would be only too willing to fleece a poor gambler.

Crooked dice

It was inevitable that unsavoury folk would adapt the roll of the dice to their purpose, by literally making crooked dice that rolled as they wanted them to. The Museum of London has in its possession a most curious little item that shows that dice-tricksters were thriving and presumably plying a lively trade in the Sixteenth Century. It consists of a small pewter pot that was found buried in centuries old silt on the north bank of the River Thames, near to London Bridge. When cleaned up they found an engraved double-headed eagle within a shield. Inside it was 24 small dice, and not one of them was an honest one.

Figure 7: *A set of 24 Elizabethan crooked dice were found in the mud of the River Thames in London.*

Eighteen of the dice were loaded. X-rays revealed small bored holes containing mercury which made them fall a certain way. These would have been known as 'Fulhams', since the Thames-side village of that name was notorious for dice-tricksters. Eleven of these 18 would land as a five or a six, while seven would land as a one or two.

Three others were 'high men', which means that they only had the numbers six, five and four on them. And the remaining three were 'low men' with only one, two and threes. These work on the principle that only three faces will show at a time. A practiced dice-trickster could easily palm and replace honest dice for his chosen crooked ones.

Yet it was a risky business for flogging in the public pillory with the crooked dice strung round one's neck was one of the penalties for being caught with such dice. Habitual offenders could expect a one-way trip to the gallows.

Judge Bridlegoose and the law of dice

The French doctor and writer Francois Rabelais (1483–1553) wrote a series of five satirical novels collectively known as *The Life of Gargantua and of Pantagruel*. They are both giants, Gargantua being the father of Pantagruel. He introduces a character called Judge Bridlegoose who explains that a successful lawyer must spend long hours with hefty legal tomes and showily unfold lengthy documents if he wished to reassure a client. Then when they are not looking he simply throws a dice, for it is as sure a way of deciding a case as any. His logic was that both sides had a chance of winning and over a number of cases he would be bound to get the right result in half of his cases. It was less anxiety and less dithering for him and it seemed as good as the law could get.

Interestingly, there are echoes of this in Luke Rhinehart's cult novel *The Dice Man*, written four centuries later in 1999. In this a bored psychiatrist allows the dice to decide his choices in life. If you have not read this novel, I heartily recommend it.

The Compleat Gamester

In 1674 William Cotton published an instructional book about all the games that could be played in his time. Very usefully he also included accounts of all the different methods that hustlers and tricksters would use. He described the High Fulhams and Low Fulhams, that I have described earlier, and also described various other types of crooked dice and means of controlling the way they rolled. We shall be covering much of this in later chapters, so that you can detect if someone is gaining an unfair advantage in a game.

The New World and beyond

Early travellers to the Americas introduced dice and dice games to the Native Americans and in that they proved a truism, that exploitation quickly follows exploration.

As the country was gradually settled, gambling and dice games proliferated everywhere. Mining camps, boom towns on the cattle trails, railroad junctions and developing cities all proved ripe ground for saloons, gaming houses and casinos to develop and thrive. The Mississippi, Ohio and Missouri riverboats spread the cult and soon dice were rolling all over the country. And even though there have been episodes when they were well-nigh outlawed, they have never stopped.

MODERN DICE

There are now a huge variety of dice available. Before I describe the different shapes and types let us consider some basic dice structure. It may surprise you, but there is more to this than you might imagine.

Standard dice – East and West differences

It is worth fishing out whatever dice you have in the house and examining them as you read this. If they are ones that were included in a game they will be either made of wood or plastic. They will be cubes with their sides numbered with dots from one to six. The dots are usually indented, or they might just be painted on. We call these 'shop dice' in the UK and 'candy-store dice' in the USA. Very often they will have slightly rounded edges, which helps them to roll when played on a variety of surfaces.

Most dice in games measure about half an inch square, although you can get them half that size and others two or three times as big.

Most people are aware that the numbers on two opposing faces add up to seven. This has been the basic design of dice since about 1400 BC. This little fact is used again and again in various dice tricks and we will come to look at this in the chapter on Dice Magic.

Less well known is the fact that dice can be right or left-handed. This is a topological principle that may interest the mathematically minded of you, in that right-handed and left-handed dice are mirror images of each other, but they cannot be superimposed on each other.

As I mentioned earlier, crooked Fulham high dice will have six, five and four repeated, but because you will only see three faces at a time when a die is resting on a surface, you will not notice. We shall use that three face visible phenomenon to look at handedness of the dice.

Figure 8: *Right and left handed dice.*

Because the opposing numbers add up to seven, it means that the one, two and three and the six, five and four will meet at opposite vertices. Get a die in front of you and check that out. Now place it in front of you so that the six is on top and so the five and the four are also visible. Western die will have the four on the left and the five will be to the right of it. That is, it goes counter-clockwise. This is called a right-handed die. It is the standard pattern of all western dice. If you set it so that the one, or the ace, is on the top then the two will be on the left and the three on its right.

Chinese dice are left-handed. A left-handed die with the six on top will have the four on the right and the five on the left. With the one on top it will have the two on the right and the three on the left of it. That is, it is clockwise. You will see this on Mah Jong dice.

Look at the pips now. There are differences here also. Western dice tend to have all the pips either black or white. They are all the same colour and the same size.

Chinese and Korean dice have a single very large one or ace, which is coloured red. And the four is also usually red. There is an interesting legend

---

Most shop dice are a bit crooked

You might not think it, but they are. These standard dice are not precision made and they will be slightly weighted more to the five and six because they have more indentations in them so they are lighter. This crookedness may not be apparent until you have had a lot of rolls. Try just rolling and recording the rolls 100 times and see (if you have the patience!)

about why the Chinese dice are arranged thus, although there are different versions as to when this occurred. One version says that the emperor in question was Lo Ling Wong, the fourth emperor of the T'ang dynasty who ruled from 684–701 AD. The other version says that it was an emperor who ruled during the Ming Dynasty (1368–1643). Whichever it was, if indeed it has any basis in historical fact, the emperor was playing the game of Sugoroku, a game akin to backgammon. He was losing, but had a chance of winning by throwing fours. He duly did and was so glad that he ordered the fours to be forever coloured red, like the one. And red is considered a lucky colour in China.

In Japan both right and left-handed dice are made, but as with Chinese dice the one is large and red while the other pips are black.

In Pakistan the dice are right-handed like the Western dice, but they have a large single red one and a red six.

There are two more differences between Western and Chinese dice. Both relate to the pips. Firstly in the West the pips are generally flush with the surface, whereas in Chinese dice they are indented. This is most noticeable with the single one or ace pip. The last difference relates to the way that the pips are arranged on the faces. In Western dice the two has the pips arranged diagonally at the corners, whereas on Chinese dice the two is either horizontal or vertical. And the sixes are spaced out on Western dice, but compressed on the Chinese dice.

Figure 9: Western and Eastern dice, Eastern dice in the middle.

Precision or casino dice

The shop dice are inadequate for professional gambling, because there are potential discrepancies in roll and potential to introduce crooked dice into a game. 'Casino perfect' or 'precision dice' are, as the name suggests, made to exceedingly demanding precision standards. They are hand-made to a tolerance of 0.0005 of an inch, so that there is an equal chance of them falling on any face. The pips are drilled out then filled with coloured paint of exactly the same weight as was removed. The faces are flushed and the edges are sharp with no rounding.

Figure 10: Photo of casino dice.

Casino dice are usually ¾-inch square (although sometimes they are ⅝ or $^{11}/_{16}$ of an inch, but they are always uniform sizes), in red transparent plastic with white pips. Other colours may be used. Since the 1970s many casinos use casino dice with serial numbers imprinted on them.

The early casino dice used in the 1920s were made from cellulose nitrate, but it was found that after years they suddenly degenerate and collapse. Since the 1950s cellulose acetate has been used, which is more durable. This is of most relevance to the dice collector, since casino dice do not last long in play. A set will only last eight hours then be removed from play.

The pip pattern is variable. The commonest is solid, but there are also bird's-eye spots, bull's-eye spots, ring-eye spot or intricate.

Casino dice are by definition used in casinos and they are the ones you will get to play with at any casino in the world. You will also need to obtain a set of casino dice if you wish to attempt dice-stacking, or have a go at dice control which we will cover in separate chapters later on.

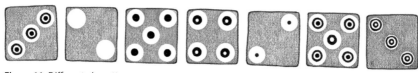

Figure 11: Different pip patterns.

Speciality dice

Dice other than the modern six sided cubes are used in a variety of games. A lot of war games and fantasy role playing games use a variety of different dice, all the way up to 100-sided zocchihedron. Usually the faces will have Arabic numerals or specific symbols relating to the type of game being played.

Standard dice notation
The standard dice notation used indicates the type of dice needed in any game. The small letter 'd' is used to designate 'die' or 'dice'. This is followed by the number of faces, e.g. d6 indicates a six-sided dice. A numeral preceding the d is used to indicate the number of dice needed in any game, e.g. 2d6 means that two six-sided dice are needed. I will be using this when we come to the games section.

Figure 12: The Platonic Solids.

The most often used dice are Platonic Solids. This refers to the shapes of the regular polyhedrons that were first described by the ancient Greek mathematicians and usually attributed to Plato. These are; the four-sided tetrahedron, the six-sided hexahedron or cube, the eight-sided octahedron, the 12-sided dodecahedron and the 20-sided icosahedron.

The Platonic Solids and the universe
Plato (428–348 BC), the great mathematician and philosopher, was the founder of the Academy in Athens. He believed that the universe was made up of minute building bricks, effectively atoms of the elements earth, air, fire and water, as first postulated by another philosopher, Empedocles. Thus: Tetrahedron (Fire), with four sides; Cube (Earth), with six sides; Octahedron (Air), with eight sides; and Dodecahedron (Water) with 12 sides. There is a fifth, the Icosahedron with 20 sides.

Plato felt that these shapes would be compatible with the qualities of the elements, since a six-sided cube could stack into a solid structure, like Earth; the 12-sided dodecahedrons and 20-sided icosahedrons would slip and slide past each other like Water; the sharp, spiky four-sided tetrahedrons would sting like Fire; and the eight-sided octahedrons would slip, slide and bounce off each other like Air.

The tetrahedron does not roll well and one can see why the traditional six-sided cube became the standard. The octahedron is the next most popular in games. The dodecahedron and the icosahedron are both used in the novelty Magic 8-ball (depending on size) which we shall consider in Chapter 9 on the subject of Dice Divination.

Role-playing games use other irregular shaped dice, some of which are more like throwing sticks and cylinders than dice. You will find spheres, cylinders, rounded prisms, tops, kites and variants with different geometric shaped faces. And they go all the way up to the 100-faced Zocchihedron, named after its creator Lou Zocchi.

I mention these variants in passing, since they are not really used in the standard dice games that we consider in this book.

Poker dice
[Standard dice notation 5d6]

These are certainly of interest, since they can be used to play poker. A poker dice set consists of five dice with the cards Ace, King, Queen, Jack, Ten and Nine on the faces instead of numbers. Five normal standard dice can be used instead, if you designate them from one, then six down to two, to represent the order of A, K, Q, J, T, N.

The aim is simply to build as good a poker hand as you can. Each player is allowed three throws, but they can stick at one or two throws if they feel that they have a good enough hand. After each throw a player sets the dice he wants to keep in his hand aside and throws the rest. Once everyone has thrown, the player with the highest hand wins. It is a game that can be gambled on for matches, counters or hard money.

Figure 13: Poker dice.

The hierarchy of hands is as follows:

- Five of a kind, in which Aces are high and nines are low
- Four of a kind, in which Aces are high and nines are low
- Full House, consisting of three of a kind and a pair, the three of a kind being the main indicator
- Straight run, the highest card taking dominance
- Three of a kind
- Two pairs, the highest pair taking dominance if another player also has two pairs
- One pair, the highest wins

Novelty dice

These may be of interest to dice collectors, of whom there are many throughout the world. Many games have been adapted to the dice, rather like poker, for example, golf and cricket.

Figure 14: Spherical and cricket dice.

Cyber dice

The internet is a fact of life these days. What a wonderful invention it has been, touching virtually every aspect of life. The word virtual is quite apposite in terms of this book, for you can now play all kinds of gambling game in cyber-space. Cyber dice or gaming with dice on the internet is proving big money for many internet casinos.

If this is your thing, so be it. Just be aware that virtual dice will be just as uncontrollable as their good old fashioned physical cousins.

Chapter 3

High Rollers and Bad Losers –
Some Tales of the Dice

Triumph depends on a roll of Fate's dice; the ultimate prize is a place in Heaven.
Friedrich Nietzsche

Ancient gamblers

It is highly likely that wagers were made on the board games that I described in Chapter 1, yet dice were undoubtedly used in all manner of other gambling games which demanded the luck of random throwing rather than skill.

The Romans were passionate about dice, but because they were aware of the risks to discipline that could follow gambling they passed several laws during the time of Augustus. One stated that if someone permitted gambling with dice to take place in his home he was barred from pressing a suit against anyone who may have cheated him. Most significantly, there was a law that prohibited dice gambling except during the festival of Saturnalia, when dicing was practiced with total abandon. During this week-long festival in honour of the god Saturn there was much drinking, feasting and general merrymaking. Even slaves were allowed to gamble.

If we want examples of the ways that Romans flaunted the laws we need look no further than the emperors themselves. Several of them were ardent dice players. Augustus himself was addicted to gambling and Domitian, Commodus, Claudius, Caligula and Nero were all enthusiasts.

Caligula (12–41 AD), the ruthless emperor who almost certainly suffered from schizophrenia, loved to gamble. His reign was characterised by horrific excesses and eccentric behaviour, such as making his favourite horse Incitatus a senator. He hated to lose at dice and it is said that he was not above having wealthy citizens arrested on trumped up charges and executed so that he could claim their wealth to pay off his gambling debts.

His successor, his uncle Claudius (10 BC–54 AD), himself a prolific historian and writer actually wrote a book, which is sadly lost to posterity, on *How to Win at Dice*. It is recorded that he even had a carriage specially designed with

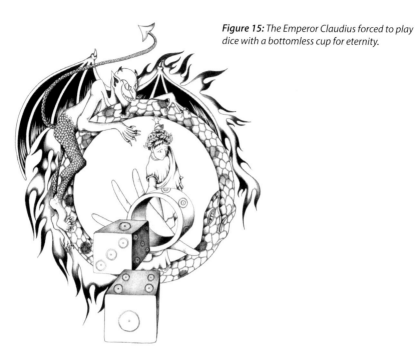

Figure 15: *The Emperor Claudius forced to play dice with a bottomless cup for eternity.*

a balanced table inside so that he could play dice whenever he was travelling. The dramatist Seneca satirised him and portrayed him in hell, forced to play dice with a bottomless cup for eternity.

His step-son Nero (37–68 AD), the famous emperor who fiddled while Rome burned, would bet up to 400,000 sestertii (about £400,000 or $650, 000), on a single throw of the dice.

An island at stake

In the *Heimskringla*, or the Chronicles of the Kings of Norway, there is a book entitled *The Saga of Olaf Haraldson*. It tells of King Olaf who ruled Norway between 1015 and 1030 and who became Saint Olaf, the patron saint of Norway, after his death.

For some years there had been bitter disputation and war between Norway and Sweden until the kings met and agreed that there should be peace between the two countries. Then it was pointed out that there was doubt about the ownership of the island of Hising. Now that peace had been established they agreed to decide the fate of Hising by playing a game of dice, the highest thrower claiming the prize.

First the King of Sweden threw two sixes and said that it was futile for Olaf to throw since he could not win. Olaf insisted and threw two sixes as well. Again the King of Sweden threw two sixes. This time Olaf threw, but one of the dice split in two. The good die came up six and the two halves of the split dice came up showing a one and a six, making Olaf's throw a thirteen.

Accordingly, Olaf won Hising for Norway.

Richard the Lionheart

King Richard I, known as Coeur de Lion, the Lionheart, spent very little of his reign in England, believing that his purpose in life was to wage a holy crusade to gain back the Holy Land. During the First Crusade in 1190 he passed a law which prohibited dice playing by anyone below the rank of a knight. Yet in order to curb gambling debts and teach his knights to practice moderation they were not allowed to lose more than 20 shillings a day. If anyone did, and was found out, then they had to pay a forfeit of one hundred shillings.

Curiously, this law did not apply to either King Richard or King Philip of France.

The Wars of the Roses

This is the name given to the period of dispute about the throne of England by two noble houses, the House of Lancaster and the House of York.

King Henry VII, who won his throne from King Richard III at the battle of Bosworth Field in 1485, was a notorious dice player. His accounts record various losses to the royal purse as a result of his gambling pursuits.

For a par of tables and dise bought, 1s. 4d
To Hugh Denes for the Kinges pley at dice upon Friday last passed, £7. 15s
To my Lorde of York to pley at dise, £3. 6s. 8d

It is interesting that despite the wicked and dissolute reputation that King Richard III gained, mainly due to the play by William Shakespeare, there is no record of him having been a gambler.

Bluff King Hal

Historiography is the name given to the way that history is told. It is a bizarre fact that King Henry VIII, the monarch who had three of his six wives executed, oversaw the Dissolution of the Monasteries and toted up a tally of some 72,000 executions during his reign, should be affectionately known to posterity as Bluff King Hal.

Figure 16: *King Henry lost the bells of St Paul's in a dice game.*

What is not so well known is the fact that he was a gambling addict and that he was an avid dice player. Indeed, he lost the bells of old St Paul's Cathedral and a great deal of money scheduled for the construction of Westminster Abbey through the unkind roll of the dice.

Good Queen Bess

Queen Elizabeth I is equally fondly remembered in history; as Gloriana, the Virgin Queen, or Good Queen Bess. Why exactly she evoked such fond memories is unclear, since she was as culpable in the deaths of many of her subjects as were her ancestors. She sent her cousin, Mary Queen of Scots, to the block and also had many nobles and former favourites, like Sir Walter Raleigh, executed in the Tower of London.

Queen Elizabeth enjoyed playing dice, having been taught by her sister, Mary, known to history as Bloody Queen Mary.

The sad case of Antonio Rinaldeschi

In Florence on 11 July 1501 a young man by the name of Antonio Rinaldeschi was playing dice in the Fig Tree tavern close by the Piazza dei Alberinghi. He had lost not only his money, but also some of his clothes and he was in a foul temper. As he walked across the piazza he cursed the name of the Virgin and threw some horse dung at a fresco of the Madonna in a tabernacle on a side wall of a church.

There was public outrage and several days later he was found in the gardens of a Franciscan convent outside Florence. Realising the strength of public feeling against him he tried to commit suicide by stabbing himself in the chest with a dagger. It was not a fatal blow, however, the blade having struck and bounced off a rib. He was taken back to Florence and imprisoned to await trial before the committee of magistrates, known as *Otto di guardia*, the Eight of Security.

He was found guilty of sacrilege and begged the court to execute him promptly in order to avoid being lynched by the mob. He received absolution for his crime and was hanged from the window of his prison.

Maracco the Thinking Horse (1586–1606)

In 1452 the tenancy of a public house in London's Fleet Street was given by a man called John French to his mother. This was to become the famous Bell-Savage Inn, which was a famous tavern and playhouse from the Fifteenth Century until 1873. It was burned to the ground in the Great Fire of London of 1666, but was immediately re-built.

It was also for a while home to Maracco the Thinking Horse, a gifted animal that had been trained by William Bankes a showman in the Phineas T Barnum league who took London by storm.

Bankes had been a retainer in the household of Robert Devereaux, the Earl of Essex, who had at one time been a favourite of Queen Elizabeth I, until finally falling out of favour with her in 1601, when he was found guilty of treason. The Earl was duly executed on Tower Green, going into history thereby as the last person to be beheaded in the Tower of London.

Bankes exploited his connection with his former master's family. He had a good knowledge of horses and purchased a bay horse, which he called Maracco, after the morocco leather that saddles were made from. He trained the animal and exhibited him at various inn-theatres, including the Bell-Savage, which was to be his principal venue in London.

Maracco could walk on two legs, fall and play dead on command. Other tricks involved drinking a bucket of water, then promptly urinating a full bucket on command. Apparently he also had the ability of being able to pick out the maids from the harlots in the audience, much to the anxiety of the female spectators and the amusement of the bawdy crowd.

It was his other skills that most amazed people. Bankes had silver horseshoes made for Maracco, who could count out many things by thumping his silver clad hooves on the ground as he counted.

Large dice were thrown and he would count out their value. He was never wrong. He could also kick the dice, as if throwing them himself, and count out their value. It was a fine trick when so many enjoyed the game of Hazard.

Bankes and Maracco then travelled abroad and exhibited in Paris, where Bankes was arrested on suspicion of witchcraft. He only escaped when he revealed that he had trained the horse by the use of hand-signals. They swiftly moved on to Orleons, where unfortunately, he was once again arrested when it was rumoured that Maracco was possessed by a spirit and that Bankes was a powerful sorcerer. This time both he and Maracco were sentenced to be burned at the stake.

Somehow Bankes persuaded the authorities to let him give one last performance to redeem himself. During this performance Maracco knelt down before the cross that was being held by a priest in the audience, which was taken as a sign that he was not possessed by an evil spirit. Not only were they released, but they were given money for the troubles they had endured.

Bankes died a happy, merry innkeeper in London in 1641.

The adventures of Simplicius Simplicissimus, the vagabond

This is a German picaresque novel written in 1668 by Hans von Grimmelshausen. It is set during the Thirty Years War and concerns the adventures of a young lad who joins the armies of the warring sides, turning his allegiance when it suits him.

The book is in five parts and there is a wonderful description in chapter 20 of book 2, of men playing with crooked dice. Learning the nature of the various dice along with the art of deception formed part of the charismatic life of the young Simplicius Simplissimus's colourful life. We will look at this again in the section on crooked dice.

Samuel Pepys and Sir Isaac Newton

Isaac Newton (1642–1727) was born at Woolsthorpe Manor in the county of Lincolnshire on Christmas Day 1642. A sickly child, he was to become one of the foremost scientific geniuses of all time.

He made countless discoveries and conducted innumerable meticulous experiments across a whole range of scientific disciplines including optics, fluid dynamics, mechanics and astronomy. Among many other things, he actually invented the reflector telescope.

His genius was his mathematical ability. He took the subject as far as he could and when it proved unable to help him with his research he even invented a whole new branch of mathematics, which we now know as calculus.

Every schoolboy and schoolgirl know that after seeing an apple fall from a tree he came up with the theory of gravity. We can actually date the time that this occurred as being sometime in either 1665 or 1666. We can work this out because Plague had broken out in London and fears of its spread were rife. Cambridge University, where he was working, was closed down to limit spread of the disease, so he returned to Woolsthorpe Manor. It was during this time that he described seeing the apple drop from a tree in the manor garden.

This was the germ of an idea that he developed into his gravitational theory, which he published in his famous three volumes *Philosophia Naturalis Mathematica Principia* (Mathematical Principles of Natural Philosophy) in 1687. It is usually just referred to as *Principia*.

Samuel Pepys (1633–1703) was a naval administrator and Member of Parliament for Harwich during King Charles II's third parliament, which was known as the Cavalier's Parliament, since there were so many Royalists in it. He became famous after his lifetime when the diary he had kept from 1660–1669 was published after his death. In it he gives a wonderful description of life in London during the days of the Great Plague of 1665 and the Fire of London of 1666.

Pepys was elected a fellow of the Royal Society in 1665 and served as president from 1684 to 1686. He therefore was president when Newton's *Principia* was published, and his name is on Sir Isaac Newton's personal copy of the first edition of this historic book.

Samuel Pepys was clearly a colourful character, as is shown by a reading of his diary. He liked wine, women and play. He was also fond of a wager.

By contrast, Sir Isaac Newton was an irascible short-tempered man who seems to have been short on humour and jealous of his academic and personal reputation.

Dice link the two men in what has become known as the '*Newton-Pepys problem*'. It came about when Pepys wrote to Newton for advice about a wager on dice. Pepys wanted to know which of three propositions would be most likely:

- Six fair dice are tossed independently of each other and at least one six appears
- Twelve fair dice are tossed independently of each other and at least two sixes appear
- Eighteen fair dice are tossed independently of each other and at least three sixes appear

Pepys thought that the third option would be the likeliest and he needed to know, because he had a wager that this would be so.

Newton replied in three letters, which have been preserved and published. He told him that the first option would in fact be the likeliest and he gave him a logical outline of why. He then gave a detailed reply using his new mathematical method of calculus. It showed that the first proposition was likelier than the second and that the second was likelier than the third.

Pepys accepted the proposition and in colourful language apparently said that he proposed, therefore, to welch on the wager!

Deacon Brodie – the model for Dr Jekyll and Mr Hyde

Edinburgh in the Eighteenth Century was not a city conducive to a healthy life. Countless thousands lived within a few hundred yards of Edinburgh Castle. The Royal Mile extends from Edinburgh Castle to the ruins of Holyrood Abbey. For centuries narrow 'closes' or alleyways led off either side of The Royal Mile in a herring-bone fashion. These were enclosed within the city walls and as the population of the city increased, so the buildings were extended upwards. Indeed Edinburgh had the first skyscrapers in the world, some of the buildings in the closes extending to 14 storeys. When no further upward building was possible, they dug down into the sandstone to create the network of underground closes that effectively became the underground city.

It is almost impossible to believe the squalor that people lived in during the Sixteenth and Seventeenth Centuries. These closes were built so close together that they were literally only feet apart. And when you think that some of them rose to 14 storeys, then clearly people living in the lower floors had next to no daylight. The poor who were forced to live underground had no light at all. There was no sanitation. All waste was hurtled into the close with a cry of 'Gardy-loo' preceding it. This was to give anyone passing an opportunity to cry back 'Haud yer haun' (hold your hand, or wait a moment), or receive the bucket of waste. But in any case it is said that one would expect to walk ankle deep in raw sewage on the bottom of the close.

William Brodie (1741–1788) was born into a family of cabinet-makers and inevitably became one himself. A highly skilled craftsman he rose to become a member of the town council and the head of the guild of Wrights and Masons, earning himself the title of Deacon. The fashionable families of Edinburgh were soon employing his services to make cabinets and furniture and he became a pillar of the community.

Yet despite his position and the comfortable living that he made, yet there was something about his personality that craved baser adventure. By day he was respectability itself, but at night he was a frequenter of the lowliest of

Figure 17: Deacon Brodie.

taverns, a gambler with loaded dice, and a philanderer. He had two mistresses by whom he fathered six illegitimate children, neither mistress knowing of the existence of the other.

It is thought that his needs for money exceeded his ability to earn it legitimately, so he started burgling houses he had worked in. Eventually he formed a small gang and planned an armed raid on an excise house in Cannongate. But the affair was botched badly and his fellow thieves were soon caught. One of them turned king's evidence and the hunt went out for Deacon Brodie, who fled to the Netherlands with the aim of taking a boat to the Americas. He was caught and arrested before he could board the ship and taken back to Edinburgh and tried.

Brodie and his fellow gang member, George Smith, were sentenced to be hanged. It is alleged that Brodie's friends fitted him with a steel collar and that he actually may have cheated the hangman on the gibbet, for his friends took custody of his body and there is no record of a burial. Some suspect that his friends, one a lawyer and the other a doctor, revived him and aided him to take passage to the Americas after all.

We will never know whether Brodie's final throw of the dice was successful or not. Yet Robert Louis Stevenson immortalised him in his dark novel about the polarity of the personality, *The Strange Case of Dr Jekyll and Mr Hyde*, set in that claustrophobic atmosphere of Edinburgh's Royal Mile.

Crockford's of London

Regency London saw an explosion of interest in gambling and gaming among all classes.

William Crockford had started his working life as a fishmonger, but saw an opportunity in other men's willingness to gamble. He brought his knowledge of odds to the betting table, however, and soon outplayed those he gambled against. He bought a share in a small gambling den and reputedly won a quarter of a million pounds in a 24-hour gambling session. He then set up Crockford's in 1793 where the rich, powerful and the celebrated came and indulged.

The club was known as a place where fortunes could change on the roll of the dice in the games of Hazard, or the turn of the cards. People such as the Duke of Wellington, Lord Chesterfield and even Benjamin Disraeli could be seen there. Yet although it was a place frequented by the pillars of society and was luxuriously furnished, it was disparagingly referred to as 'The Fishmonger's', a slight on William Crockford's humble beginnings. He himself was portrayed in cartoons as 'The Shark'.

Crockford spoke with an East End accent and was not ashamed of his origins. Indeed, he seems to have cultivated the appearance of someone who was less intelligent than he was. In truth, he knew that his mathematical ability was greater than that of most of his clients. Shrewdly he ensured the loyalty of his staff by allowing them to share in the profits. In 1827 he moved into spacious and luxurious premises in St James Street. He employed Louis Eustache Ude, a brilliant chef, so that soon Crockford's was a place to dine as well as to game.

Hazard was the dice game of choice and in 1827 he spent £2,000 in dice alone. The centre piece of the whole building was the Hazard table, a simple piece of mahogany covered in green baize. For years William Crockford would sit in a corner of the room, watching play at that table, aware that his entire fortune was made by the repeated roll of dice upon it.

He died in 1844. He had amassed a fortune, but lost a great deal of it. His personal vice had not been the roll of the dice, but business speculation. It was not something that his mathematical ability could bend to his will.

The Great Chicago Fire

Chicago is situated on the south-western tip of Lake Michigan in the state of Illinois in the USA. The city was built around the narrow River Chicago in 1830 and, with the building of the railroad, it soon became the main transport centre for livestock and grain from the mid-west. It became known as the wooden city and it was because of this that a disaster was liable to happen.

The summer of 1871 had been both hot and dry, so the ground was parched and the timber buildings were like kindling. On a Sunday evening a fire broke out in a barn belonging to Patrick and Catherine O'Leary. Firefighters were called, but unfortunately were sent to the wrong neighbourhood, with the result that when they did arrive at the barn they found the fire out of control. The conflagration spread north and east and raged for two days. It devastated the city, causing three hundred deaths, made one hundred thousand people homeless and caused a staggering two hundred million dollars worth of damage.

Catherine O'Leary was made a scapegoat in an article by the *Chicago Tribune*, which said that the fire had been caused by one of her cows kicking over an oil lamp. Over the years the story of the Great Chicago Fire became the object of much speculation and investigation. In 1893 Michael Ahern, the reporter who wrote the cow and lantern story, confessed that he had fabricated the story. Yet still various other theories continued until in 1944 a man called Louis M Cohn died, leaving a letter with his will. In this he confessed to having been playing craps in the barn with James O'Leary, the son of the barn's owners, Daniel 'Pegleg' Sullivan and some others. At an exciting point in the game, an oil lamp was knocked over and the fire raged instantly. Gathering up the money they all beat a hasty retreat.

John 'Big Jim' O'Leary went on to run saloons, casinos and gaming houses in Chicago and died a very wealthy man. Louis M Cohn also died a man of considerable substance, bequeathing a considerable sum to the Northwestern University's School of Journalism.

Chapter 4

Dice Lore

As dice are to be wished by one that fixes
The Winter's Tale, Act I Scene II
William Shakespeare

All gamblers are superstitious. It seems that they have been throughout time. It is perhaps not surprising with regard to dice, since they were the tools of the shaman, as we saw in Chapter 1. As such it was believed that their very roll was under the influence of the gods.

The Greeks venerated Tyche, generally regarded as a guardian goddess of cities, overlooking their prosperity. She was usually depicted carrying a cornucopia and a wheel of fortune.

The Romans worshipped her equivalent as Fortuna. A golden statuette of her, also depicted with a cornucopia and a wheel of fortune, was constantly kept in the sleeping quarters of all of the emperors.

Contemporary gamblers know her as Lady Luck. She has appeared in many guises in popular culture; as a socialite crime fighter in a comic of the 1940s, as a part in films, books, and as a song in the musical *Guys & Dolls*. She is often portrayed in emerald green, with her hair garlanded with four leafed clovers and with lucky dice ear-rings.

Gamblers may not actually worship her in a religious sense, yet they will often invoke her aid through some aphorism, ritual, charm or talisman.

Gambling superstitions
Four-leafed clover, rabbit's feet, glass Whitby ducks and all manner of little figurines of leprechauns, pots of gold and even little dice on key-rings are testimony to the fact that gamblers believe in that mysterious quality called luck.

Gambling can be addictive. More than that, it can be a dangerous addiction, which causes people to gamble fortunes away, notch up debts and lose not only the fabled family kitchen silver but the kitchen and the whole house as well. If someone has a win then they often subconsciously try to recreate the situations that led to that win. It may be that they were wearing a particular

Figure 18: Lucky 7-up dice, four-leafed clover and lucky elephant good luck charms.

article of clothing, standing in a particular place, or that they went through some little ritual beforehand. In the developing gambler's mind that can result in a set of mental associations being set up. The ritual, the charm in the pocket, the favourite gambling shirt may all become incorporated into the magical thinking that is so linked up with the belief in luck.

What is magical thinking? Well, it is something that psychologists have done much research into. It is a way of thinking that we all have as children and which some people never lose. It is a way that we try to understand the way that the world works, especially those phenomena that do not seem to have any logical explanation. Effectively, we infer that there is a sort of magic principle at work. It is almost as if an individual will ascribe some of this magical power to an inanimate object like a charm, or a special ritual, such as touching your ear three times, in readiness to influence some course of events. If it seems to work then the belief is reinforced.

Craps playing has attracted almost as many of these little superstitions as those that surround poker playing. Let's have a look at a few.

Never disturb a good roll – if someone is having a good roll then bad luck will occur if it is disturbed by anyone throwing money on the table to cash in on their luck.

Don't use the word 'seven' when someone is playing – this is a bit like actors never directly referring to the play *Macbeth*. Instead they call it 'the Scottish play'. At a craps table you call seven 'it' or even 'the devil'.

Don't touch anyone on a good roll – it is bad luck to do so. And further, don't speak to them unless they speak to you.

The Virgin Principle – there is no such thing as being PC in craps lore. This is the belief that a woman who has not played craps before will have a good roll the first time she plays.

Beware the Male Virgin Principle – a male first timer is not good luck. No one will expect him to win and so will not bet when a first timer is rolling.

A strike means a seven is coming – if a die hits someone's hand then it is believed that a seven will follow on the next roll.

When dice leave the table a seven is coming – if a die shoots off the table, then it is believed that a seven will follow on the next roll.

Fool's folly to be first – no one wants to be the first to roll. It is believed that the dice will be cold and that they need to warm up.

Don't throw when the dice showing seven are presented by the stickman – it is considered bad luck. This is so well known that you are unlikely to be given this by a professional stickman.

Wrong betters make a seven more likely – this means people who regularly bet against the shooter are more likely to make a seven turn up.

Blow life into the dice – when a shooter begins it is common to blow good luck into the dice. Yet this is considered unhygienic these days. It is not to be encouraged!

There are logical explanations for some of these which have less to do with luck than with simple mathematics and odds. Once again, this is such an important area that the subject of odds deserves a chapter all to itself. I would suggest that if you are a dice and gambling novice, please read that chapter before you try your hand at the craps table or indeed any type of dice gambling.

One Last Chance – a gambler's tale

'Pah! Another evening of straight losses at the table,' the dandy in the bottle green jacket complained. 'Lady Luck has deserted me again. She let the devil turn the dice and with them my last dollar.'

He drained his brandy, snapped the glass down on the bar then moved through the crowded smoky atmosphere of the gaming room and headed outside into the night air.

A fairly dense fog had fallen and the lights along the side of the great vessel seemed watery and strangely distant. The noise of the engines thrummed and the great paddle wheel was churning the water with a relentless ruthlessness, shoving the riverboat down the Mississippi.

He pulled out a long cigar from an inner pocket and struck a light to it, puffing until the tip glowed red. He patted his pocket and felt the heavy presence of his derringer. It had two chambers, but just the one bullet. He had carried it every day for just such a time as this – when he had nothing left to live for.

'Even my last cigar,' he mumbled morosely to himself as he moved towards the rail to allow a couple to sidle past. He watched them disappear into the mist.

Absently, his hand went to his waistcoat pocket and he drew out the pair of silver dice that he had carried ever since the day he found them and decided to become a professional gambling man. He shook them in his fist and then opened it to see if she had a final message for him.

'A three and a four!' he mused. 'Are you telling me something Lady Luck?'

He did not expect to hear an answer, yet one came, clear and distinct from behind him. A woman's voice.

'Three!'

He spun round expecting to see someone, but there was nothing. Just an empty walkway. The mist swirled about him.

'And four!'

He spun again, almost feeling dizzy as he did so.

But again there was no one there.

His brow broke out in sweat and the dice in his hand seemed to burn. Almost involuntarily he tossed them into the night and heard them plop into the water below.

'– makes seven!'

'Who's there?' he demanded, pulling the derringer from his pocket and holding it before him at arm's length. 'I'm armed.'

The mist swirled and he thought he saw a figure advancing slowly towards him.

'St…Stop! I'll shoot.' His hand was shaking badly.

'Shoot who?' he heard the female voice whisper a few inches behind him.

He staggered side-wards, trying to keep an eye on what he thought was the advancing figure as he edged his head round to see if there was anyone there.

'M..Myself,' he stammered, raising the derringer towards his temple.

The figure seemed to solidify in front of him. Seemed to come straight at him.

Instinctively he pointed the gun at the figure and fired.

The explosion echoed into the night and was drowned by the relentless churning water of the paddle wheel. A breeze caused the mists to clear and he realised that there had been no phantasm. No advancing figure.

'Your last chance. Don't waste it.'

Then he was alone.

Chapter 5

Crooked Dice

The devil is in the dice

Old English proverb

From what you have read so far it should be quite clear that ever since dice started to be used in games, both gambling games and straight games for leisure, people have wanted to give themselves an edge in order to win. Some people have tried to develop a skill in the way that they throw the dice, yet others have used nefarious means by introducing crooked dice into whatever games they were playing.

In Chapter 2 on the history of dice I described the set of Fulhams that were found in the mud of the River Thames and which are now housed in the Museum of London. As you may recall they were called Fulhams because the Thames-side village was notorious for dice-tricksters in Elizabethan England.

Important note
Cheating is illegal, potentially dangerous and definitely not nice! The intention of this chapter is to help you spot when someone may be cheating. It is for your interest and protection only.

In Chapter 3 on High Rollers and Big Losers I mentioned the book *The Adventures of Simplicius Simplicissimus*, in which the hero describes the various types of crooked dice used by dice tricksters. Let us hear what he had to say on the subject:

Among the false dice were Dutch ones, that one must cast with a good spin; for these had the sides, whereon the fives and sixes were, as sharp as the back of the wooden horse on which soldiers be punished: others were High German, to which a man must in casting give the Bavarian swing. Some were of stag's-horn, light above and heavy below. Others were loaded with quicksilver or lead, and others, again, with split hairs, sponge, chaff, and charcoal: some had sharp corners, others had them pared quite away: some were long like logs and some broad like tortoises. All which kinds were made but for cheating: and what they were made for, that they did, whether they were thrown with a swing or trickled on to the board, and no coupling of them was of any avail; to say nothing of those that had two fives or two sixes or, on the other hand, two aces or two deuces. With these thieves' bones they stole, filched, and plundered each other's goods, which they themselves perchance had stolen, or at least with danger to life and limb, or other grievous trouble and labour, had won.

This is a wonderful description written five hundred years ago, yet the principles of the crooked dice that were used then are still practiced by magicians in the legitimate pursuit of their art, which is entertainment, and less wholesomely by dice cheats. Nowadays professional dice cheats are known as 'dice mechanics', and if you ever chance to indulge in a game of dice played for money outside a legitimate casino, then you are potentially at risk. It is the aim of this chapter to warn you about the things that you should look out for so that you can protect yourself against being cheated by a dice mechanic.

Honest dice

There are several names for these. Straight, square, perfect or level: that is, they are undoctored and will fall on each face one in six of the times.

Or they should!

Honest dice are often a little crooked!

This is simply a matter of the weight of paint on a die. If the die is an accurate cube then the six-face will have six times as much paint as the one-face. Since the four, five and six will meet at a vertex there will be a tendency for these numbers to show slightly more frequently than the one, two and three. It may not be a huge difference, yet it will probably be enough to stack the odds in a gambling game. Have an awareness of this.

Honest dice may behave as if they are crooked

This is an interesting phenomenon you should be aware of when you play with two dice. It is also worth knowing because if you are ever offered to gamble on the way that numbers come up you could lose a lot of money.

You might care to try this with a couple of dice just to demonstrate to yourself that this is real.

Suppose I say to you that I bet you even money that I can roll a one or a six on every roll of the dice. Let us say that we will do it over ten rolls. And just for interest let us say that you wager $5 a roll.

If you try it you will very probably find that you have lost a fair amount of money over a very short time.

At that point you might think that there is something about the one and the six. In that case choose any two other numbers, say a three and a five. Do it over another ten rolls and you will see that you are again down by a similar amount.

This is all to do with odds. I am going to cover this in a separate chapter, but it is appropriate to consider this little phenomenon here since it is a way that honest dice could be used in a crooked way.

Each die has six numbers so there is a one in six chance of any number coming up with each die. You would think that you had only two chances in six of throwing your two chosen numbers on each occasion. In fact, you have a five in nine chance. That is quite enough for someone to win a neat little pile and beat a hasty retreat.

Think about it. If you have two dice, a white one and a black one, there are 36 possible combinations. There are 20 that will show at least one die having one of your two numbers. That is 20 combinations out of 36, making it a five in nine rather than the two in six that you imagined.

Have a look at Figure 19, showing the 36 combinations, and you will be able to check that this is so with any two different numbers.

Loaded dice

Loaded dice are heavier on one side, having been tampered with in some way. The heavier face will tend to fall to the table to cause the lighter side to show face up. It will not happen all the time, but it will affect the odds.

The commonest way to create loaded dice with opaque shop dice is to bore a hole or holes under the spots and add a small amount of metal, like lead or gold. Mercury has been used for this purpose for centuries, as evidenced by the weighted dice in the exhibition at the Museum of London.

You might think that transparent dice, such as the precision dice used in casinos would be failsafe, but even those can be doctored. You will not find loaded dice in a casino unless they have been switched by a crook. Even that is highly unlikely because tables are watched by experts.

Be wary of any dice being used for gambling outside a casino. Even precision casino dice can have their spots removed, weighted and then be replaced to look perfectly innocent.

Floaters

These are dice which have been tampered with, but instead of being weighted, they have had a small segment removed so that there is a hollow chamber under one face. The net effect is the same as with a loaded die; the heaviest face will tend to fall towards the table.

Two tests for loaded dice

The water test – get a tall glass of water and gently lower the die into the water. Do this several times changing the face on top each time. If the die swivels and shows one face more often that the others, it is a loaded die.

The pivot test – hold the die diagonally between finger and thumb and gently relax pressure. Repeat this to test all four vertices. If it swivels it is loaded.

Tappers

These are dice which have had a clever little cylindrical or dumb-bell shaped chamber hollowed out, one end being at the centre of the die and the other being near one of the faces at a corner. This is filled with a bead of mercury and the face is made to look innocent. When the mercury is at the centre it will behave like an innocent, honest die. When the crook gives it a tap on the appropriate corner before throwing centrifugal force shoots the mercury towards the corner, so it will behave as a loaded die.

One should watch out for a gambler tapping his dice on the table before throwing, even though he has assured you he is touching the table for luck.

Shaped dice

Obviously if a die is not a perfect cube it will roll erratically, which may alter the odds enough to make a difference – particularly if the dice swindler knows which number it is biased towards.

A die can have one faced shaved down, so that it is effectively like a short brick. This is called a '*brick*' or a '*flat*'. This will have the effect of always tending to land on the shaved-down side or its opposite face, because they are both square shaped whereas the other faces are rectangles, which will have a smaller surface area on which to land. The commonest type is called a '*six-one flat*', when either the six- or the one-face is shaved down. This could work against the shooter in craps.

Two way flats are when two different (not opposite) faces have been tampered with. Thus if six and three are shaved, then the six, one, three and four will appear more frequently. If two dice have been prepared like this then sevens will show up more frequently.

Other combinations can be created, depending on what a dice swindler aims to bias the throw towards.

Bevel dice are ones that have the edges of a face very slightly curved rather than properly edged, so that they will roll on the bevel and not land on that face, thereby biasing the die. To test them lay two dice against one another and rub them; if they 'wobble', there is a bevel.

Split edged or **saw-toothed** edges have a few tiny notches on an edge so that they will grip.

Capped dice have been shaved down and the face capped with another material that will be more elastic than the other faces, so that it will bounce off that face.

Mis-spotted dice

These are dice which have faces mis-spotted so that they do not conform to the standard.

Double number dice have one number repeated on opposite faces. For example a '*double deuce*' die has two twos and no fives.

A pair of mis-spotted dice with one, five and six on one die and three, four and five on the other will never produce a two, three, seven or twelve, which are losing numbers in craps.

'High-low splitters' are dice which have been prepared so that one is a high die with six, five, and four repeated, while the low die has one, two, and three repeated. They work on the principle that only three faces are ever visible, so that they could be switched into a game to devastating effect. They will produce a lot of sevens.

How to identify mis-spotted dice

Because they only have three numbers which are repeated, the die will appear to go the right way fifty per cent of the time and the wrong way the other fifty per cent. That is, one way it will seem to be right handed, and the other way it will be left handed. Check this out by getting any box and drawing the mis-spotted dice numbers on it. You will see what I mean.

Electric dice

These are dice prepared with magnetic metal spots or a metallic face. So that a strong electromagnet built into a table could make the die show the desired number at the flick of a switch.

It is to be hoped that you never find yourself in a situation where you are playing with dice that have been tampered with. There are manufacturers who can supply these, so be warned. Your best safeguard of course is never to play dice for money with strangers. Finally, if you do find yourself in such a situation, be careful about challenging someone. If they are dishonest enough to swindle you they may be capable of becoming quite nasty. Just cash in your chips or excuse yourself from the game.

Chapter 6

Odds and Probability

If the odds are a million to one against something occurring, chances are 50–50 it will.

Unknown quote (but the odds are that someone will know!)

T his is a really important chapter that anyone contemplating gambling with dice should have a look at. The thing is that although the dice are capable of giving much entertainment, the fact is that certain combinations of numbers are more likely than others. You need to know about probability and about odds.

Luck

We had a little look at this in the chapter on Dice Lore, but we need to consider it in more detail here, because so many people believe that they are touched with more luck than their fellows. Gamblers are particularly prone to this belief and no amount of losing or parting with hard earned cash will persuade them otherwise.

People often describe luck as an actual thing, or as a kind of mystical energy that they can feel. When someone 'feels lucky' they may take a chance on something, speculate on the stock market, or put their money on some event or game. Quite what this lucky feeling actually feels like is far harder to pin down. It seems to amount more to a belief than to an emotion or a physical sensation. Sometimes people will respond to a suggestion in a horoscope or a fortune cookie in a Chinese restaurant that the signs are propitious or that Lady Luck is smiling on them, and off they go and have some sort of a flutter.

It is the idea that one is being singled out that tends to make people believe in luck, whether that is good luck or bad luck. When you roll a streak of winning dice at craps against the odds and you scoop a packet of money, you will almost certainly believe that you have been lucky. Similarly, if you blow all your money on a series of losing bets, then you are liable to think that you have been unlucky. The simple fact, however, is that because something is unlikely to happen, does not mean that it won't. Take the National Lottery, for example. Although it is generally reckoned that your chances of scoring the winning line and hitting the jackpot is said to be one in many, many million, that does not mean that you have to have many, many million goes at it in order to win once. The thing is that there will be many, many million people betting on the same lottery and among them one or more people will win. You might even win at the first attempt – if you are lucky!

To put all of this into context, it is not at all surprising that someone wins every week. It is logical that they should. What would be more surprising is if no one won for several weeks. Ultimately someone will select all of the winning numbers and they will scoop the jackpot.

Yet winning the lottery is simply that. It is a lottery and no system will shorten your odds of winning, apart of course from increasing the number of lottery lines that you pay for.

Being lucky at dice can be something that seems very real, yet as I told you in the last chapter in the section 'H*onest dice may behave as if they are crooked*' this is not the case. If you have skipped that chapter and come straight here, please just go back to it and perhaps try it out.

The point is that you can seem to be lucky or unlucky with dice if you bet on particular combinations, since some are more likely to come up than others. This is all to do with the branch of mathematics that is called probability theory. Know it and understand it and you will understand why bookmakers and casino proprietors are liable to prosper and their businesses always thrive.

The gambler's fallacy

This is something that you may have experienced yourself while playing any board game with dice. After a few throws when you are trying to achieve a particular number to land on a square, it just seems likely that your chosen total is bound to come up. Well it will eventually, but it is not bound to happen just because it hasn't happened up until that point.

The gambler's fallacy is the incorrect belief that in a series of independent identical events, such as the roll of two dice, the events have a fixed probability which is related to the previous results. In other words, with two dice, the probability of them landing in a particular way is the same each time. The fact that two sixes, for example, have not come up for 20 throws does not make them more likely on the next roll.

Science, mathematics and dice

The old game of Hazard, which we shall consider in more detail in the section on dice games, focused men's attention on the fact that some combinations seemed to occur with more regularity than others. Richard de Fournival (1200–1260) was a medieval philosopher and the chancellor of the cathedral chapter of Notre Dame d'Amiens. In a poem called *de Vetula* he described the ways that some combinations were more common than others.

In 1564 mathematician, physician and passionate gambler Girolamo Cardano[1] (1501–1570) wrote the first ever book on probability, *De Ludo Aleae*. In it he wrote about dice and knucklebones.

Galileo Galilei (1564–1642), the astronomer, mathematician and physicist who was one of the first men ever to use a telescope studied the way that dice fell. He was consulted by a wealthy nobleman who wanted to know why in Hazard the number 10 came up more frequently than nine. Galileo experimented with dice, finding that with two dice there are six multiplied by six, that is 36 possible combinations that can be made. If you have three dice, then there will be six multiplied by six multiplied by six, that is 216 possible combinations. Of these, there are 27 ways that 10 can be made up, but only 25 ways to make nine. Quite enough of a difference to cause a lot of money to change hands if you bet on the wrong combinations!

In the mid Seventeenth Century a flamboyant gambler, the Chevalier de Méré had won a considerable amount of money by betting that a six could be thrown with a single die at least one in four rolls. He could not understand why with two dice a double six would not come up at least once in 24 rolls. He asked the mathematician and philosopher Blaise Pascal (1623–1662) to investigate.

Pascal corresponded with Pierre de Fermat[2] (1601–1665), a lawyer and amateur mathematician famous for his work on the theory of numbers. After a lengthy exchange of letters they concluded that with 24 rolls there was a slight but definite advantage of not rolling a double six, but that if 25 rolls were made the advantage would swing the other way. Between them they laid the foundations of probability theory.

In 1657 Christianus Huygens wrote the first book on probability *De Ratiocinniis in ludo aleae* (Reasoning in Games), outlining the way that dice fall.

Probability

Some folk hate the very mention of mathematics. Yet don't worry, I am not going to go into any great detail here. I am merely going to illustrate a few points that may help you avoid being caught out by a hustler.

Probability is the number of times an event occurs divided by the number of times it could occur. Thus, for a single die to be rolled, there is a one in six, expressed as $1/6$ chance of it showing any one of its six faces.

Probability is expressed as a number between zero and one. It is a sort of fraction. If an event is impossible, its probability is stated to be zero. If an event is certain, its probability is one.

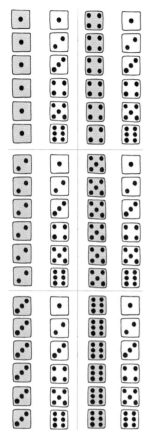

Figure 19: The 36 combinations with two dice.

Simple so far, is it not?

Let us go back to the honest dice hustle I talked about in Chapter 5. Get two dice of different colours. Now I want you to roll the dice and see if you can roll either a one or a six. Do it a few times and you will be surprised at how often one of them comes up. Now do the same with a three and a four. Again, it almost seems as if you are making it happen.

Look at Figure 19. You will see how I have laid the dice out. Now, simply start at the top left and go down combinations, then start at the next row and go down, counting each time you have one of the two numbers. Don't recount if you have both numbers or a double, because you have already counted that as a combination. You will find that you have 20 possible combinations out of a possible 36 combinations. That means that you have a $^{20}/_{36}$ probability of rolling at least one of the two numbers each time. You can cancel that down to simplify the probability to $^{5}/_{9}$.

Odds

These really do seem to be mysterious numbers don't they? If you look at betting figures on any sporting event it seems as if the numbers are plucked out of the air by the bookmaker. Well, yes they are, and no they aren't.

Is that confusing?

What I mean is that the bookmaker is in the business of making money, just as are the proprietors of any gambling establishment. There is not a casino anywhere in the world that is based upon philanthropic principles. They are willing to let you bet with them, they give you a chance to win, but you can be utterly certain that the odds are in their favour.

Right, what is the difference between probability and odds?

Simply this, if the probability of throwing a six with a single die is $^{1}/_{6}$, the odds *against* it are 5/1. That is there are five chances of it being another number against one of it being a six. Odds are the chances for something not happening against the chances of it happening. Thus it can be odds in favour of something or odds against it happening.

If you have a probability of ½, it is described as being fifty-fifty. Then the odds are fifty per cent one way and fifty per cent the other.

If you have a one in 36 chance of throwing a double-six with two dice, the odds against throwing a double-six are 35 to 1.

You get the idea?

Percentage

I just said that sporting events will attract odds. That is you are given a chance to place a bet according to those odds. They may seem tempting, but the chance is almost always stacked against you. That is, you have far more chances of losing your money than you do of making a handsome profit.

For one thing, on most events it is a rule of thumb or a guesstimate that is being given, not a precise mathematically calculated probability with a corresponding odds figure. The guesstimate is made and then it will probably be adjusted in favour of the bookmaker or betting agency.

It is not just that the figures speak for themselves (which they should do now), but that the bookmaker or casino take a percentage. In respect to casinos the 'percentage' is often referred to as the 'house edge.'

You will undoubtedly have heard these terms bandied around on TV, in films and by gamblers. They will say things like 'there is no percentage in that', meaning there is no advantage for them. Or they may ask, 'what is the percentage in it for me?'

'What's the edge?' In other words, what advantage can I take?

Effectively, a bookmaker or casino expects to make a percentage profit on each event. You can see this with horse races, football, and of course at the various events on offer at the casino.

Putting it very simply, however much money is taken in bets, less should be paid out to winners. If you bet on a fruit machine, it may have a 95 per cent payout percentage.

That may not be bad, you think, but it means that you are never going to get an even bet. Some portion of your winnings may be kept back so that the house wins even when it loses. And if you bet frequently, you will lose.

Some betting games have more of an edge than others. The old favourite The Wheel of Fortune played in fairgrounds and available in some casinos has a house edge that varies according to the bet, up to a staggering 27 per cent. You do not need to play that for long to lose money consistently.

With all dice games played for money always think in terms of odds and probability if you want to at least go home with the money you started with.

Also be sure you know what the house percentage is before you do any sort of gambling.

Craps

I am going to run through the game of craps in a separate chapter of its own in the game section, but we will just consider some very basic probability that you ought to be aware of before you venture near a craps table. You may find it useful to read this section and then skip ahead and read the chapter on craps to get it all into perspective.

Basically, in craps the 'shooter' is the person who is currently throwing the dice. Only one shooter throws at a time and up to 20 people can play the table at a time. The commonest bet is a 'pass bet'. This means that you win if the shooter throws a 'natural'. That is a combination of seven or 11 on the first roll. You lose if a 'crap' is thrown. That is if two, three or 12 is thrown instead.

If the shooter had thrown a four, five, six, eight, nine or 10, then that number becomes his or her 'point'. The shooter continues to throw until either the point is rolled, when he will win, or a seven is rolled, when he will lose.

You can see now how crooked dice can be used to win a game, if they are switched in by sleight of hand during a game.

Now look at Figure 20. This again shows the 36 possible combinations of two dice, but assembled in a different way. Once more they are coloured differently to show the combinations. Of course, in a game they would be the same colour!

Note the numbers down the left side of the column. The first number shows the combination sum. The second column shows the number of ways the sum can be made. The third column gives figures in brackets, which are the percentage probabilities of making that combination sum[3]. For example, two and 12 can only be made one way in each case, so the probability of rolling then is only 2.78%. By contrast, seven can be made by six possible combinations, so it has a probability of 16.67%.

Now if we look at the pass bet. The probability of making a natural seven or 11 is 16.67% for a seven, plus 5.56% for 11. That means that you have a 22.23% chance of making a natural to win. On the other hand, a crap would be 2.78% + 5.56% + 2.78% (respectively for a two, three, or 12), which makes 11.12% to lose.

Brilliant, you might say. That means that on the first throw the shooter has twice as much chance of throwing a natural to win than of throwing a crap to lose. The downside of this is that when you add up the other numbers; four, five, six, eight, nine or 10 (which would make up a point), that he has to hit:

$$8.33\% + 11.11\% + 13.89\% + 13.89\% + 11.11\% + 8.33\% = 66.66\%$$

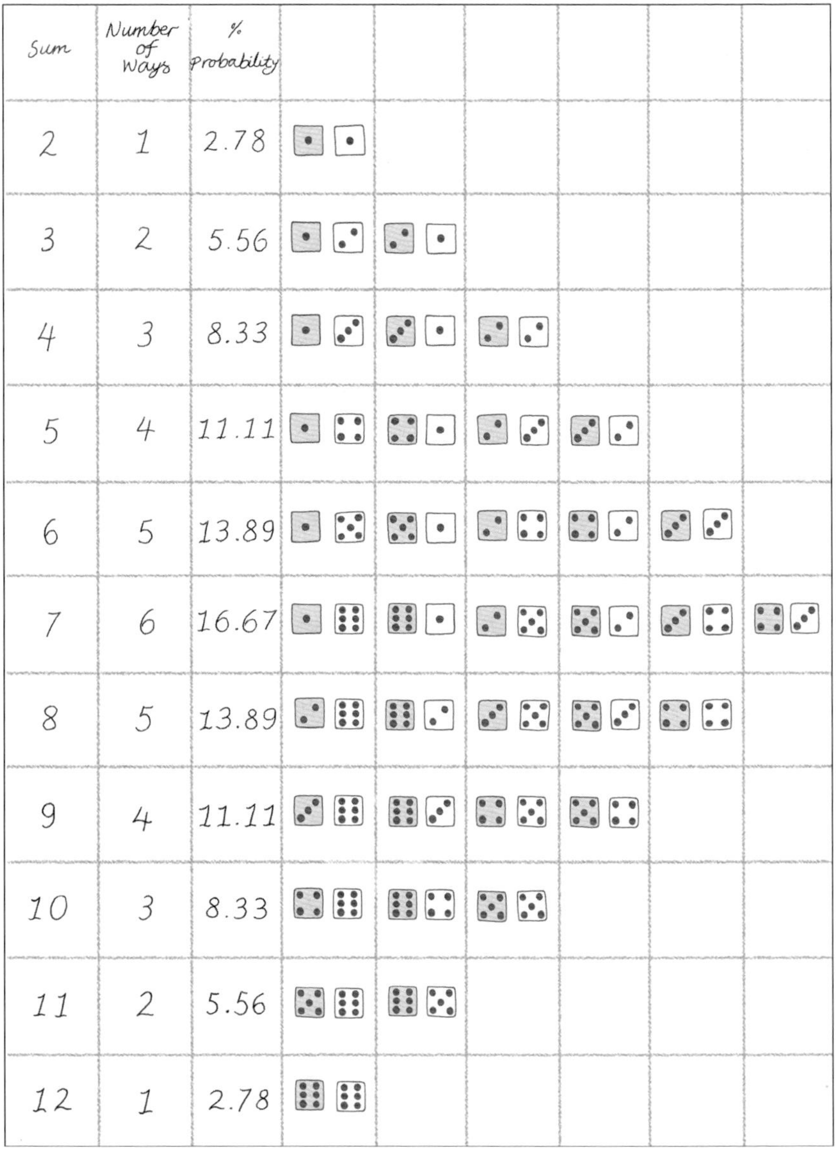

Sum	Number of Ways	% Probability									
2	1	2.78	⚀ ⚀								
3	2	5.56	⚀ ⚁	⚁ ⚀							
4	3	8.33	⚀ ⚂	⚂ ⚀	⚁ ⚁						
5	4	11.11	⚀ ⚃	⚃ ⚀	⚁ ⚂	⚂ ⚁					
6	5	13.89	⚀ ⚄	⚄ ⚀	⚁ ⚃	⚃ ⚁	⚂ ⚂				
7	6	16.67	⚀ ⚅	⚅ ⚀	⚁ ⚄	⚄ ⚁	⚂ ⚃	⚃ ⚂			
8	5	13.89	⚁ ⚅	⚅ ⚁	⚂ ⚄	⚄ ⚂	⚃ ⚃				
9	4	11.11	⚂ ⚅	⚅ ⚂	⚃ ⚄	⚄ ⚃					
10	3	8.33	⚃ ⚅	⚅ ⚃	⚄ ⚄						
11	2	5.56	⚄ ⚅	⚅ ⚄							
12	1	2.78	⚅ ⚅								

Figure 20: The 36 combinations of 2 dice in craps.

That means that although the shooter is twice as likely to throw a natural than a crap, he is three times more likely to throw a point. The significance of this is that then he is more likely to throw a seven than any other combination, since there are six ways that can be formed. With the chart you can see how hard the game can potentially be, and how hard it is for the better to win.

Correct odds in craps

If you do venture into a casino to play craps the house will decide the odds. These are likely to be advantageous to the casino, since they are a business and their purpose is to have an edge.

Just remember that the correct odds for throwing the sum totals are:

The sum	Correct odds
2 or 12	35 to 1
3 or 11	17 to 1
Any 7	5 to 1
Any crap – 2, 3 or 12	8 to 1
4 or 10	11 to 1
6 or 8	6.2 to 1
5 or 9	8 to 1

Odds against making a point before a seven

Now this is important in casino craps. Don't just depend on blissful ignorance and Lady Luck! Be forearmed, or just be prepared to hand your money over.

From Figure 20 you know that a seven can be made in six ways. Also from the illustration you can see that a four or a ten can be made in three ways. Therefore the odds against throwing a four or a 10 before a seven are 2:1.

Thus, the correct odds against making a point before a seven are as follows:

The point	Number of ways	Correct odds
4 or 10	3	2 to 1
5 or 9	4	3 to 2
6 or 8	5	6 to5

Games with multiple dice

It should be clear that the more dice you bring into play the greater the number of combinations possible. With three dice, there are 216 combinations ($6 \times 6 \times 6 = 216$); with four dice, there are 1,296 combinations ($6 \times 6 \times 6 \times 6 = 1296$); and with five dice there are 7,776 combinations.

Because of the greater number of combinations, the probability of hitting particular combinations becomes less and less. For example, to throw a three or an eighteen with three dice (three ones or three sixes) the probability is only 0.46%, because there is only one way that you can throw either of these totals. That means $^1/_{216}$, which as a percentage is 0.46%. To throw a 10 or 11 with three dice can be done in 27 ways, giving a probability of 12.50%. That is considerably less than the chance of throwing a seven with two dice.

When you get to five dice, the probability of throwing a five or a 30 (five ones or five sixes) is down to $^1/_{7776}$, which as a percentage is only 0.01%.

For more detailed information please have a look at Table 1 showing the probabilities for three, four and five dice. Simply note that as you move from left to right the probabilities increase.

You can see how knowing about odds will help.

FOR THREE DICE – top row numbers, mid row combinations, bottom row probabilities (When three dice used 216 possible combinations)

3/18	4/17	5/16	6/15	7/14	8/13	9/12	10/11
1	3	6	10	15	21	25	27
0.46%	1.39%	2.78%	4.63%	6.94%	9.72%	11.57%	12.50%

FOR FOUR DICE – top row numbers, mid row combinations, bottom row probabilities (When four dice used 1296 possible combinations)

4/24	5/23	6/22	7/21	8/20	9/19	10/18	11/17	12/16	13/15	14
1	4	10	20	35	56	80	104	125	140	146
0.08%	0.31%	0.77%	1.54%	2.70%	4.32%	6.17%	8.02%	9.65%	10.80%	11.27%

FOR FIVE DICE – top row numbers, mid row combinations, bottom row probabilities (When five dice used 7776 possible combinations)

5/30	6/29	7/28	8/27	9/26	10/25	11/24	12/23	13/22	14/21	15/20	16/19	17/18
1	5	15	35	70	126	205	305	420	540	651	735	780
0.01%	0.06%	0.19%	0.45%	0.90%	1.62%	2.64%	3.92%	5.40%	6.94%	8.37%	9.45%	10.03%

Poker dice

This game can make people forget that they are playing with five dice, because it is played with special dice each bearing the image of a playing card; Ace, King, Queen, Jack, Ten and Nine. It is a game that people will gamble on, so it is worth having some idea of the probability of throwing particular combinations.

To throw five of a kind with five dice, probability of $^1/_{1296}$, or odds against it are 1295 to 1

To throw a specific five of a kind with five dice, probability $^1/_{7776}$, or odds against it are 7775 to 1

To throw four of a kind with five dice, odds against it are 51 to 1

To throw three of a kind with five dice, odds against it are 5.5 to 1

To throw any two pairs with five dice, odds against it are 3.3 to 1

To throw any pair with five dice, odds against are 1.2 to 1

To throw any full house with five dice, odds against are 25 to 1

To throw a specific full house with five dice, odds against are 777 to 1

In poker dice you can retain one or more dice and then throw again to make up a hand. The following are the odds of making certain hands.

If a pair is kept and three are rolled, then the odds of making the following hands are:

Five of a kind	odds against are 215 to 1
Four of a kind	odds against are 13 to 1
Three of a kind	odds against are 1.2 to 1
Full house	odds against are 5 to 1

If three of a kind are kept and two are rolled, then the odds of making the following hands are:

Five of a kind	odds against are 35 to 1
Four of a kind	odds against are 2.3 to 1
Full house	odds are 1.25 to 1

If four of a kind are kept and one is rolled, then the odds against of making five of a kind is 5 to 1.

Sucker bets

This is just a word of warning. Unless you fully understand the principles of probabilities and odds with dice, do not be tempted to go for any bet that is not straight-forward. It could be a sucker bet, meaning that you have little or no chance of winning and you will part with your money. It does not mean that they are dishonest, it is just that you are being persuaded to bet against probability and the probability is that you will lose frequently and perhaps quite a lot.

Sucker bets are used in private dice games and you are probably as well to avoid them, because there is no one to regulate them except the players. If there is a hustler present, and you probably will not be aware of it, then you will lose. No one announces that they are about to hustle you, after all.

Know also that there are sucker bets in casinos. When I come to describe craps in the games section I will include some sucker bets that you should be aware of. They relate to the layout of the craps table and to the way that you place certain bets.

Forget the systems

So many gamblers spend a lot of their time trying to discover a system that is going to help them to buck the system or break the bank so that they can retire to a life of luxury. The thing is that there is no system that will do that. If you have picked up this book in the faint hope that I can supply you with such an elusive phantasm then I am sorry to disappoint you. I do not believe that any credible system works and if you are minded to gamble, then simply take on board what I have said about probability, understand it in relation to the activity you are pursuing and bet cautiously.

The Martingale system is the most popularly known. It came into vogue in France in the Eighteenth Century. Essentially, you place modest amounts on the surest bet. If it comes up you place the same modest amount on the next bet. If you lose, you double your next bet. If you lose again you double it yet again, and so on. When you do win, you go back to the original modest wager.

There is another, called the Rothstein system, which is basically the same. It favours the safer type of bets in craps, the pass bets. Essentially the first bet is to place one unit; if it wins you are one unit ahead. You keep betting one unit at a time only. If you lose, you then bet double the first bet plus one, so you bet three units. If you lose that you double up and add one again, so you bet seven units. And so on.

The truth is that neither work. This is because you are always betting against a house percentage, and the simple fact is that the more you bet the more you pay in house percentage cumulatively. Also, the house will have a betting limit, so that when you hit the losing streak, which you will, then you will be increasing so much that you will probably exceed the limit and not be allowed to bet, so you cannot recoup your losses.

This is not to say that you cannot ever win. You can, but it is not through using a system. It is through understanding probability and odds, and betting strategically.

Notes

1. Girolamo Cardano wrote the first description of the infectious disease Typhoid fever
2. Pierre de Fermat is famous in mathematics for Fermat's Little Theorem, but perhaps even more so for what has come to be called Fermat's Last Theorem.
3. These figures are derived by turning the probability fraction into a percentage. For example, $1/36 \times 100 = 2.78\%$ and $6/36 \times 100 = 16.67\%$

Chapter 7

Dice Magic

Hocus pocus
William Vincent[1], Court juggler and conjuror
to King James I of England

Conjuring is one of the oldest of the performing arts. *The Westcar Papyrus* from 1500 BC, now in the Berlin Museum, tells tales of magic and conjuring, performed at the court of King Khufu, the builder of the Great Pyramid. One of the five tales relates to a performance for the pharaoh by a magician called Dedi. Many books on the history of magic refer to this performance (although in some he is referred to by the names Tchatcha-em-ank), during which he decapitated a fowl and then restored it to life (fear not, this is a trick that is still done by street magicians and the bird is never harmed). It is also suggested that he was the first magician ever to perform the trick known as the cups and balls.

A wall mural dating from 2000 BC, from the tomb of Baqet III at Beni Hassan, a small village not far from Cairo, is said to depict a conjuror performing this ancient trick.[2]

It is outside the scope of a book devoted to dice to delve too far into the history of the conjuring art, beyond saying that people in all cultures since

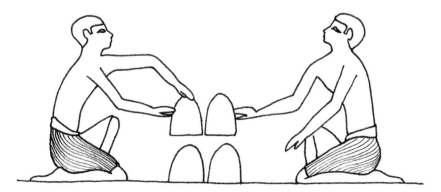

Figure 21: The cups and balls in ancient Egypt?

recorded history began have enjoyed being amazed and made to think that they are seeing magic. Dice have always had a conjuring connotation and it is therefore entirely appropriate to devote a small chapter to some simple conjuring tricks that are entertaining, effective and easy to perform.

Magic Tricks

In keeping with the traditional way in which conjuring tricks are set out in magic books I am going to set these little gems before you in the following format:

Effect – a brief description of what the audience sees
Method – the secret and the way of doing the trick
Presentation – a suggested patter and way of performing the trick

The Three Magic Words

These are not Abracadabra, or Hocus pocus, although using such words may be useful in your presentation of a trick. Very simply, to be effective as a conjuror you need to Practice, Practice, Practice! Use a mirror to see what it looks like. Rehearse the trick and the patter until it becomes second nature. Then when you do present your trick, it will be most effective if it seems off the cuff. And do not repeat it, no matter how much people ask you to do so. It is far better to be able to follow it up with a different trick, so that you have a mini-repertoire to show them. Repetition gives a spectator a chance to see how you did it.

The magician's code

This is something that all serious conjurors try to adhere to. Simply, keep the secret of the trick to yourself.

THE DISSOLVING DIE

If you remember, I began this book with a description of a magic trick that I first obtained many moons ago when I was six years old. It is one that requires some preparation, but it is an effective one to amuse youngsters.

The Effect

A die with a hole bored through it is displayed. Two cords or ropes have been threaded through it. The ends of the top rope are knotted to secure the die. The ends of the ropes are then grasped, two in each hand and at the utterance of a magic word the ends are pulled. The die dissolves through the knot and the ropes and falls to the ground or a table, leaving the conjuror with the two ropes stretched between his hands. Ropes and die can then be examined for trickery.

Please see the diagrams that accompany my introduction to the book.

Method

The secret is all to do with the ropes, not the die. The preparation is all done 'offstage' before you bring it into view. Take the two ropes and double each one, then stuff the middle of the rope into the hole in the die. Push the other into the other side so that they meet in the middle. The appearance is that of a die with two ropes threaded through it.

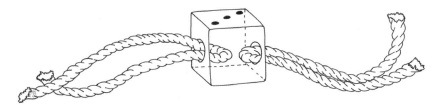

Figure 22: *The secret of the dissolving die.*

Now, in front of the audience you take the two ends of what seem to be the top rope, but which are in fact the ends of two separate ropes, and tie a simple knot on top of the die.

When you now grasp two ends in each hand and pull, the ropes simply slip out of the die and the knot will 'dissolve' to leave you with two stretched ropes between your hands.

Presentation

Misdirection is what this is all about. You show the die and draw attention to the two ropes that have been threaded through the die. You then draw attention to the 'top' rope and tell them that since you are tying a knot over the top you have ensnared the die securely between the two ropes. Then when you pull and the die drops, you tell them that the die has dissolved through the knot and the ropes. Since the two ropes will be the same length and are obviously not tricked, everyone will assume that it is the die that is tricked.

Which inspection will reveal that it is not.
Simply raise an eyebrow and take a bow.

[**Note** – if you wish, you can perform this quite effectively with a simple die from a game. Just bore a hole through its centre and use string or wool. It can easily be set up and kept in a pocket to demonstrate in close-up.]

THE PEARL-DIVING DIE

This is a little science curio rather than a magic trick, but it is the sort of little thing that can be carried in a purse or wallet and provides a little diversion every time you are asked to do a trick at a party or in a bar.

The Effect
You take out a small die from your purse or wallet, drop it in a glass of lemonade and watch it sink to the bottom. After a few moments you say the magic word and it will rise to the top. Snap your fingers and it will sink back down again, just like a pearl diver.

The Method
All you need is a small enough die. A light one, like the type that come out of crackers. Make sure it is clean and keep it clean in a little polythene bag. When you need to perform, you need a freshly poured glass of lemonade or cola, anything that has some fizz in it. Even champagne if you are celebrating, especially if you are celebrating after a win!

After suitable patter, such as below, drop the die in and watch it sink to the bottom. Keep the patter going until you see that the die has become covered in bubbles, then say the magic word and watch it float to the surface. After a few moments the bubbles will start to burst and at that point snap your fingers and it will sink as if under your control.

And you can keep going because it will continue going up and down like this.

Presentation
This is entirely due to the fact that a fizzy drink is releasing bubbles of carbon dioxide. They will form on any object in the drink and will accumulate until they have covered its surface. This then is a case of buoyancy. If the bubbles are light enough to overcome the weight of the die, then they will raise it to the surface. Once at the surface the bubbles start to burst, so the die will eventually become too heavy for the remaining bubbles and will sink.

I suggest that you start a story about winning prizes, saying something like 'who dares' wins the prize. Then talk about the pearl divers of the South Seas who are capable of diving to great depths to scoop up oysters and thereby claim the pearls that have formed within them.

Indicate that the bubbles forming on the die are like tiny pearls. Then when you say the magic word and the die begins to rise, tell them that sometimes the daring pearl divers win the great treasure, like this treasure cask that is coming to the surface.

Then when it sinks again, finish with the line, 'but course, making a living from pearl diving is a big risk. Rather like gamblers and the roll of the dice.'

THE THREE CUPS AND DICE

At the start of the chapter I mentioned that Three Cups and Balls is the oldest known magic trick. This variant is easy to learn and perform, and you are following in the footsteps of conjurors dating back to the building of the Great Pyramid itself.

The Effect

Three empty cups and three dice are placed on a table in front of the conjuror. He places one die on top of the middle cup then caps it with one cup and then caps that with the third, so that the three cups are stacked. He says the magic word and lifts the stack to show that the die has appeared underneath the cup.

He then places the bottom cup on one side, the middle cup over the single die and places the third cup on the other side. Again he places a die on top of the middle cup, then caps it with the other tow cups, then he says the magic word. When he lifts the stack there are now two dice under the cup.

Then he places one cup to the side, the middle one over the two dice and once again places the last cup on the other side. He places another die on top of the middle cup, then caps it with the two other cups. Lifting the stack this time he shows three dice on the table.

Next he puts one of the dice in his pocket to leave two on the table. He then again places one cup down on one side, then one over the two dice and the third is placed to the side. He then caps the middle cup with the two outer cups, snaps his fingers and lifts the stack to show that all three dice are together again, the third one having magically flown there from his pocket.

All three dice and all three cups may be examined.

The Method

For this trick you need four small dice of the same colour and three cups, like small painted yoghurt pots. The dice should be the smallest that you can get and the cups should have sloping sides so that they can be stacked. It is also best to have a table cover to prevent the sound of falling dice. You will see why in a moment.

You set the cups up like this. Place one cup on the table, then drop one die inside. Then lift the cup and place it inside one cup. Then place another empty cup inside the first cup. Thus you will have three cups stacked one inside the other. The die is concealed inside the middle. Drop three dice into the topmost cup.

This is ready to perform. Place the stack on a table with the three dice inside.

When you are ready to perform, lift the stack of cups up and tilt the stack towards the audience and tip out the three dice. As you do this, make sure that they see the cup is now empty. Then hold the stack perpendicularly as in Figure 23, with the mouths facing to the ceiling.

Now remove the bottom cup and tilt it to show that it is empty, but don't say anything about it being empty. This is part of the misdirection. Place it mouth down on the table.

Now the main part of the trick. Casually remove the bottom of the two remaining cups (which contains the hidden die) and turn it over to go mouth down next to the first cup. The die will not fall out and with practice this can be made to look very natural. Then tilt the last cup again to show that it is empty, but don't say anything, since this will unconsciously make the audience think that they have seen all three cups empty. Place it on the other side, so that you have three cups in a row, the middle one covering the hidden die. Take one die and place it on top of the middle cup as in Figure 24.

Figure 23: *The fourth die is hidden inside the second cup.*

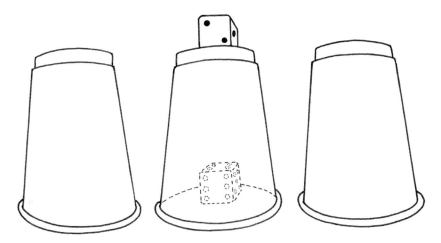

Figure 24: *Now the secret die is under the middle cup.*

Then cover it with the two others. When you lift the stack the die seems to have gone through the cup, but it is the original concealed die.

Now hold the stack perpendicular again and remove the bottom cup and place it mouth down on one side of the die. Remove the bottom of the two remaining cups (which will again hold a concealed die) and deftly invert it over the die on the table, so that it now covers two dice. Then place the third cup mouth down on the other side. You repeat the process in exactly the same way, so that you stack, then reveal two dice. Go through the whole process again and you will have three dice on the table and the hidden one again inside the middle cup.

Now you take one die and place it in a pocket. Then go through the process again so that at the end you will reveal the three dice under the cups. You can then show the three cups to be empty and take a bow.

Presentation

Tell the audience that you are a student of magic and that you were fascinated by the account of the great court magician Dedi (or Tchatcha-em-ank, if you don't mind being historically inaccurate – it is a magic trick you are giving remember, not a lecture) and that you are going to recreate that original illusion for their edification.

This trick can be performed without any words, or you can fill in the gaps as you see fit. The thing is to do it fairly quickly, for then you don't give people enough time to work it out.

And it is a very effective trick that conjurors have been performing for four thousand years. Indeed, in the archives of the Magic Circle there is a photograph of the Cups and Balls that were used by His Royal Highness Prince Charles when he performed upon entering The Magic Circle.

THE ROBBERS AND THE SHEEP

This is a variation on an old trick that you may have seen performed with pieces of paper to represent the robbers and the sheep. This one is done with seven dice of the same colour, but two of which have specially prepared. You also need a couple of boxes which represent two barns.

The Effect

There are two boxes on a table, from one of which you carefully take out and place in a row in front of the barns five red dice, which you tell the audience represent a farmer's five sheep. Then you take out two black blocks without spots to represent the two rustlers. Showing that the barns are empty you begin the tale.

One night the farmer was very worried because two sheep rustlers had been seen in the neighbourhood. He was determined to stay up and keep a watch in case they showed up. As dark fell the rustlers appeared and each one went into a barn. There they enticed the sheep in one by one, one into the right, one into the left, and so on. The farmer noticed that the sheep had disappeared from view so he sneaked up towards the barns.

The robbers then panicked and so they started shooing the sheep out again. The farmer sees them and feels relieved so he goes back to the house. Once again the rustlers started to coax the sheep into the barns, one by one.

The bleating of the sheep alerts the farmer and he marches out with a gun, fully expecting to find a rustler in each barn with some of his sheep. But when he opens the first barn door out trot the five sheep. While he is tending to them the two rustlers had somehow managed to sneak into the other barn, so they sneak out and escape.

Both barns are now empty.

Method

The trick is in the way that two dice are prepared and in the way that you handle the counting. Take two of your dice and get some black masking tape. Apply a square of it to three adjacent faces of each die. If you place it on the table, as you know from the principle of the cheat Fulham dice that I talked about in Chapter 2, you can only see three faces at a time. They will either look like ordinary red dice or like two black cubes, as in Figure 25. You can if you prefer, actually paint three faces of two dice with model paint.

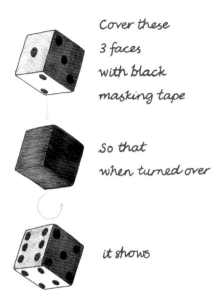

Cover these
3 faces
with black
masking tape

So that
when turned over

it shows

Figure 25: The prepared dice.

You start with all of the dice together in one box. As you take them out and lay the dice in a row, you make sure that the two rustler dice are taken out last and presented black faces to the audience.

Look at Figure 26 and you will see the handling process in three stages. The first column shows the sheep and the robbers going into the barns. The middle column shows them coming out of the barn. And the last column shows them going back into the barn again. The two specially prepared dice are marked with a cross to differentiate them.

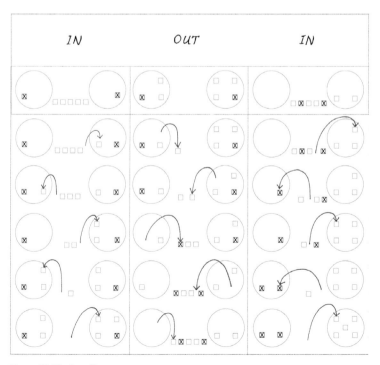

Figure 26: The handling process.

Very simply, you put the two rustlers in the two barns first and immediately turn them round so that they are ready for the second phase of the trick when you take them out disguised as sheep dice.

You see that after putting them into the barns you put the sheep in the following order – right, left, right, left, right. Thus you will have one disguised rustler in each barn, and three ordinary sheep in the right and two ordinary sheep in the left.

When you start bringing them out you begin from the left, so that you end up with three ordinary sheep and two disguised rustlers on the table, and two ordinary sheep left in the right hand barn. Everyone will think that you have still got a rustler in each barn.

When you put them back again, you do so by putting one ordinary into the right, then a disguised rustler into the left, then an ordinary sheep into the right, then a disguised rustler into the left, then an ordinary sheep into the right. You now have the two disguised rustlers in the left and the five ordinary sheep in the right.

You can tumble the ordinary sheep out of the right, then turn and lift the rustlers to show that they are rustlers and immediately pocket them to show that the rustlers have sneaked away, to rustle another day.

Presentation
You will find that if you stick to the story as described and practice the turns, that you have a very effective little trick that will convince everyone that you are adept at sleight of hand.

DICE DIVINATION
You need to be able to do a mental conjuring trick. How about this one with three dice?

The Effect
You hand a spectator three dice and get them to roll them while your back is turned. Then get them to make a stack of the three. You turn and with barely a look at the stack tell them that you can make a dice divination. You reveal a number, which will be the total of the numbers that are hidden from view.

As the top die is removed and the hidden numbers are added together, your audience will be amazed that you were correct.

The Method
When you turn you simply glance at the top number. You then subtract that from 21 and you will have the total.

After giving the total you deliberately instruct the spectator on which number to add. Firstly, he should remove the top die and look at the number on its bottom. To this add the number of the second die that has been revealed. Then lift that up and add the number that was on its bottom, then the number on the top of the last die, and finally the number on the bottom of the last die.

The Presentation
This is as outlined in the Effect. The only thing to focus on is that you only glance at the top number then quickly look away. Misdirect the audience's attention to the other numbers that are on the other faces, and the fact that you could not have seen them all.

DICE CHALLENGE
This is a neat little challenge that can drive folk mad. Is it a game of luck or logic?

The Effect
You take two dice, give one to a spectator and keep one yourself. The challenge is to take turns in showing a number that is added to a total. The winner is the first person to make exactly 50. Not 51, not 52, but 50. Challenge to best of three. But you never lose!

Method
This is just mathematics. If you allow the spectator to always go first you will always win. If he insists that you go first you will still probably win. That is because you have a secret!

The secret is in knowing that you have to aim at certain special subtotals. These are 8, 15, 22, 29, 36, 43 and 50. Essentially, each time you are give your chance to show, you show a number to hit one of these totals.

If you are made to go first, then you always start with one. That way your spectator cannot get to eight, but you will be able to next time. If you keep ahead by scoring on the subtotals, you will win, unless you make a miscalculation!

Presentation
This is all about a little hesitation. Consider; as if you are estimating a lucky number. Then show surprise when you win. Stop at three games because there is a chance that the secret will be discovered by the mathematically adept.

DICE CATCHING

Here are a number of little easy to do stunts that show you have a certain dexterity with dice, necessitating as they seem to do, fast reflexes.

The Horizontal Catch
The Effect

Figure 27: The horizontal catch.

You take three dice of one colour in a row and place a different coloured die on top of the middle die in the row. You then raise them between finger and thumb and explain that gamblers and dice experts tend to warm up by a few exercises, like this one. You aim to let the middle dice drop and catch the top one between the other two.

You demonstrate it effortlessly, yet no one can duplicate your prowess, much to their frustration.

Method

You can try to do this by continual practice, but you are unlikely to get it right even then. The secret is in simply moistening your finger and thumb at the start. Then when you grip the dice row, if you simply open your grip slightly the two end dice will stick to finger and thumb and the middle die will fall. Do this momentarily and you will find that you catch the top die in a pincer move.

Practice it well and be surprised at how effective it is.

Presentation

As with most conjuring tricks it depends on how well you misdirect your audience. Here you are misdirecting them from the fact that your finger and thumb are slightly moist. You are making them believe that it demands great skill and fast reflexes, when it is merely a trick. Sell the reflex part and they will believe that you have faster reflexes than they do after they fail repeatedly to emulate you.

Toss and Catch

This is one to follow on from the last, or you can do it first if you wish. Either way, it is another routine to frustrate anyone who tries to match you

The Effect

You take two dice and a dice cup, explaining that to warm up you need to be able to control the way you throw dice. You clip one die to the side of the dice cup with your thumb and rest another die on top as in Figure 28. You then toss one die up and catch it in the cup, then repeat it with the second so that they both remain in the cup. Your spectator will not be able to do it without the first falling out of the cup when they try to catch the second.

Method
Catching the first is easy. You flick the die up and catch it. Then when you prepare to do the second you raise the cup as if to launch the second die, but instead you bring the dice cup down quickly as you release the die and collect it as it falls. If you throw it up, the one in the cup will be flicked out.

Presentation
This is again all about telling the spectator how skilful you have to be and misdirecting him into thinking that you threw the dice up rather than lowered the cup.

Figure 28: Toss and catch.

Back of the Hand Catch
This is fun. You can do it with casino dice, but if so you are limited by the size of the dice and the size of your hand. If you use shop or store dice you can literally catch a whole armful!

Effect
You turn your dominant hand over and lay a line of dice along it, starting with the first one at the tip of the middle finger. You then flick them up into the air and catch them all in one go.

Method
Lay the dice along the back of the hand, starting with the first on the back of the middle fingernail. Start with just three dice to get the hang of the trick. Simply flick the dice in the air by keeping the elbow in one position and lift the hand quickly. Give the wrist a flick as well if you want. Then you turn the hand over, lower it and scoop the falling column of dice – and you will find that they fall as a column – into your cupped hand.

It is not difficult and it is fun. Establish your own record. You just need lots of dice and a long arm. There is no need to stop at the elbow, after all!

Figure 29: The back of the hand catch.

The Elbow Catch

This is another little stunt that is pretty well automatic. If you use casino dice you are limited again by the size of the dice and your hand, but you can probably catch four dice. If you use smaller ones then you can build quite a column.

Effect

You bend your arm and fold it back so that your hand is resting on your shoulder, palm facing the shoulder. You then build a column or tower of dice and stack them on the back of your elbow. With a quick toss and a downward sweep of the hand you catch the dice in your hand.

Method

There is no trick in this. As I said, it is almost automatic. Try with one die first to demonstrate. Get the arm in position then balance the die on the back of the elbow as in Figure 30.

Now simply sweep your hand downwards. The die will drop and as you turn your hand over, so that the palm is facing the floor, you will find that the die just drops into your hand.

Once you can do it with one die, then start building up to four.

And with those final examples of your dexterity, you will be ready to amaze your audience by going on to demonstrate dice stacking. And this requires a chapter all to itself.

Figure 30: The elbow catch.

Notes
1. William Vincent wrote a treatise *Hocus Pocus junior, the Anatomy of Legerdemain* in 1634. He performed regularly in front of King James I (VI of Scotland), and used the words *Hocus pocus, tontus, talontus, vade celeriter jubeo*, in order to misdirect his audience from his sleight of hand.
2. Although no less an authority than Percy Newberry, a professor of archaeology at the University of Liverpool and the leader of excavations at Beni Hassan in 1890–94, thought that this was the case, the latest archaeological opinion is that the two figures in the wall painting were bakers making bread.

Chapter 8

Dice Stacking

Practice makes perfect

Old English proverb

Any dice handler worth his or her salt should know how to perform a little dice-stacking. It is a technique that is half juggling and half sleight of hand. It started as a conjuring trick but has risen to become a performance art in its own right complete with its own world championships.

The basic aim is to pick up a series of dice one at a time from a flat surface using a dice cup in a series of rapid sweeping movements, so that when the cup is removed a vertical stack of dice is left. It is a showy and effective thing to see, but the truth is that the whole thing is based on a simple scientific principle

Figure 31: *Dice stacking – what you need.*

called centripetal force. Effectively, the motion of the cup throws each dice upwards so that they form into a column. Indeed, if the sweeping movement is kept up, although the dice are not being held in the cup by anything other than this force, they will not fall out. When they are brought to a halt on the surface they will hit one wall of the cup and stay in position as a stack.

There are various tricks of increasing complexity using differently coloured dice and different numbers but the above outline is the basis of it all. It looks incredibly difficult to do when you first see it performed, but most people can master the basic moves in less than an hour.

What you need

There are three main things:

1. At least four precision made casino dice
2. A dice cup
3. A smooth, generally sliding surface but not glass; this is simply too slippery.

The basic dice stack is done with four dice. Shop dice or the type you will find in most games can be used, but you will find it very difficult to learn the technique using them. Used casino dice work best because they have sharp edges and they move well.

The dice cup can be made of virtually any material, but avoid glass in case of breakage, which could be dangerous. You can buy dice cups especially made for dice stacking, or you can adapt any plastic cup provided it is of the right shape and size. Ideally you need it to have very slightly sloping sides. It should be tall enough to take a stack of four, but preferably five dice with room to spare. Its mouth should be able to accommodate four dice laid together to form a square.

Finally, the surface can be a tray or a table top. I suggest that Formica or a smooth tray be used to begin with, or the surface of a desk. As with any skill that takes time to develop, you will be clumsy to begin with and you do not want to risk scratching any furniture surfaces.

The old adage is that practice makes perfect; well, in dice stacking this certainly does seem to be the case. You will find that you soon become able to pick up dice by barely touching the surface. If you have the chance to watch experts at work, and You Tube will give you plenty of opportunity, then you will see people dice stacking from tiny surfaces, such as the face of a clock or a mobile phone.

The basic move

This does not take long to learn, but I have to admit that it can be frustrating as you begin. Most people scatter the dice in all directions and spend some time scuttling about the room collecting them. But practice will pay its rewards and you will find that once you have the basic move you will soon be able to build your repertoire.

Start by trying to pick up one die to begin with. Place it on the surface in front of you. Now grasp the cup as in Figure 32, making sure that you have your fingers and thumb in full contact with the cup. You do not do this with the cup held in the fingertips, but in a good full contact. This should be firm, but not tight. The reason is that you want the hand and cup to function as one unit. Indeed, to begin with you also want the wrist movement to be kept to a minimum. As you become more adept and you understand the process you can let the wrist become more active, but when you begin, there is a tendency to try to do everything too fast and to let the wrist flail about. That is generally what accounts for the clumsy scattering of the dice rather than a neat pick up.

Most of the movement is going to come from the elbow. Just to get an idea of the move hold the cup and with the elbow touching the side of your body just sweep it back and forth from side to side. As you do this, allow the forearm to roll slightly and you will see that the cup describes a slight arc in front of you. This is the sense of movement that you want to achieve; a sweeping back and forth, with a gentle roll of the forearm. Obviously, when you do start picking up dice you are going to be allowing the elbow to move forward as you reach towards each die in turn.

Now what you have to do is start with the cup on the right of the die (that is, if you are right handed; reverse it if you are left handed) and make a couple of sweeps back and forth before you approach the die with the third sweep. The starting position is with the cup tilted at about forty-five degrees.

Figure 32: Holding the dice cup.

But don't rush to try it. Concentrate on getting the sweeping movement right. Just imagine that the die is there for now. Keep the edge of the rim in contact with the surface and sweep it across, maintaining that contact. As you roll your forearm over so you will see that the rim rolls until it is at forty-five degrees on the other side. Then reverse the movement and roll it the other way.

Rhythm is the secret in this, not all out speed. The tendency is to try to scoop the dice up but, in fact, what should happen is that as you approach a die the edge of the dice cup will strike the bottom of the die (and you aim to attack it square on) and it will naturally be flicked up. The rhythmic back and forth movement will cause centripetal force to make the die fly as far up inside the cup as it can, and hence the more dice that you pick up the more of a stack you will create.

Once you have the rhythmic movement you are ready to pick up a die. Some people like to start beyond the dice and sweep them up in a zigzagging move gradually getting nearer to the body. I think it is easier to start near and work away from the body. The fact is that once you can do it one way, you will soon be able to do it the other way.

So, place a die on the surface in front of you and make one sweep from the right, one back, then another towards the die, rolling your forearm as usual and then sweep back and forth again. Now if you have actually picked it up you will be able to maintain that sweeping and raise the cup from the surface and sweep back and forth in the air. The die will not fall out if you have the rhythm right.

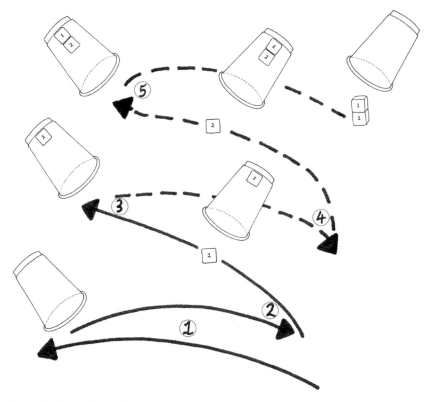

Figure 33: the two dice stack.

Keep practising this lift, and this rising from the surface, to convince yourself that you have the technique. When you want to settle it on the surface just lower and continue the sweep until you reach the end of a sweep and then abruptly stop. This will cause the die to hit the side wall and stop.

This is a forehand move, picking up on the right to left sweep, but some people feel more comfortable by doing it on the backhand, or sweeping from left to right.

Once you can do one die the next thing is to pick up a second. This really will give you a sense of achievement, because when you complete the moves, you will have one die stacked on another.

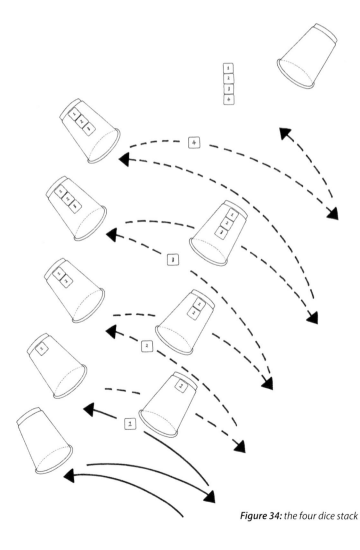

Figure 34: the four dice stack

Place two dice in front of you. When you are ready make your sweep back and forth, pick up one die, sweep back and then pick up a die on the next sweep, then make another sweep back and as you sweep forward come to an abrupt stop. Raise the cup and see the stack.

The simple truth is that if you can do a two dice stack, you can certainly do a three and then a four dice stack. My advice is to master, two, then three, before trying for four. There is nothing more frustrating than scattering a lot of dice, which you probably will if you try too hard before you have mastered the technique. But the essence of the move is all there now. My own preference is to do a sweep back and forth before beginning the whole pick up, then with the third sweep pick up one die, sweep back, then forward to pick up the second, sweep back then forward for the third, then back and forward again for the fourth; then one sweep back and another forward coming to an abrupt halt. As you lift, you should have four dice stacked in a vertical column.

You may find that you need to make an extra sweep or two in between each die pick up. It is just what you feel comfortable with as you develop your technique.

Downstacking

Once you can do the four dice stack you can move on to these more complex manoeuvres. All of them are simply variants of the basic move, but they look flashier. And if you find that you are really adept at it, you can start building your own repertoire, invent your own tricks, and perhaps even begin competing at dice stacking competitions.

This technique of downstacking involves taking a vertical dice stack and sweeping one die off at a time until you have the whole stack in your cup, which you can then lower to the surface, still sweeping as you do, so that you have effectively moved the stack from one location to another. As you can imagine this is harder than the basic move, but if you can master this then you are on your way to being a competent dice stacker.

It is purely precision; the basic move is still the same, you are simply aiming to sweep one die off the stack at a time. Obviously you are also lowering your arm with each die that you remove. Yet once again, centripetal force will do the stacking, all you have to do is the basic move. Just aim to hit one die at a time, otherwise you will scatter the whole lot.

Mixing the colours

You may already have started collecting different coloured casino dice. As a minimum you ought to aim at acquiring four dice of one colour and four of another.

Mix and match

Lay out two lines going away from you, one of red and one of green dice, slightly staggered so that you can complete your sweeps. Pick up the first four and produce an alternating stack. Then pick up the remaining four and produce another alternating stack elsewhere. Now, if you downstack from both stacks, moving from one to the other to pick up four dice, and then repeat with the remaining four, you will produce two stacks, both with two of one colour on the bottom and with two of the other colour on top. Downstack these and you will produce two stacks of the same colour again.

Sandwiches

For this one lay out a row, going away from you, of red dice and put a green die on top of each one. Then sweep off the top die of each pair and produce a stack of green. Then sweep the bottom line to produce a stack of red dice.

If you downstack from one stack you will produce an alternating stack. Then downstack the second stack and you will produce another alternating stack.

If you now downstack alternate stacks you will end up with two stacks, with two of the same colour on the bottom and two of the other colour on top. Downstack from each and you will again produce two stacks of the same colour.

The Cube into two stacks

This is a really effective one, although it is not always predictable. Your aim is to form a cube then divide the colours into two columns. It looks incredible.

Form your cube by placing two red nearest you to form the start of the base. Then place two green on the other side of them, so that you have two red

Figure 35: The cube.

Figure 36: The cube into two stacks.

nearest you and two green forming the far side of the base. Now on top of the nearest two place a red over the left die and a green over the right one. Over the far two place a red over the left one and a green over the right one. It looks as if they are mixed up (but if you can assemble them in a seemingly random manner, it looks better).

Next, turn the cube that you have formed so that it looks like a diamond in front of you. This seems to be the best way to position it. When you do your sweep try doing a backhand one first, as usual, then approach from the far right and scoop at the flat face of the cube, not the angles.

You simply sweep and do your usual sweeping back and forth several times and centripetal force should do the rest. You will have formed two columns of four dice. And if you are lucky, you will have one column of red and one of green dice.

Chapter 9

Dice Divination

*Going to the fortune teller's was just as good as going to the opera, and the cost
scarcely a trifle more – ergo, I will disguise myself and go again, one of these
days, when other amusements fail.*
Mark Twain, in a letter to his brother, Orion Clemens, February 6, 1861

Over the centuries people have used dice for divination. From the days
of the shaman right down to the current interest in all things to do
with the New Age, people have a desire for help with questions they
may have about problems in their life, or just about the future in general.

Cleromancy is the practice of casting of lots and dice. Astragalomancy is
the specific use of dice. The name derives from the astragals of quadrupeds.
There are various ways of doing it, the simplest being to ask a question, then
throw two dice to obtain a number from two to twelve. A list of corresponding
answers then gives the answer to the question. More complex methods use
three dice and a larger list of answers.

Mo divination is a system that is used in Tibetan Buddhism. The Dalai
Llama himself is said to use this technique on occasions when faced with
a difficult decision. Meditation is followed by a ritual, then the casting of a
single die twice in order to obtain an indication of the answer.

The following methods are strictly for fun, although you may find that they
give you some indications that you find useful.

The simple cast
Using two dice think of a question and then cast the dice. The total indicating
one of the following answers:

2 – no

3 – the answer is not yet available. Ask again in twelve hours

4 – there is a message on its way

5 – you are facing a financial loss

6 – yes

7 – someone has your interests at heart

8 – a journey is imminent

9 – there is potential danger ahead if you follow this through

10 – you must follow this up

11 – possibly, but you will have to sacrifice something dear to you

12 – consider the past

The Magic 8-ball

This is a fortune-telling gadget that is sold in many gift shops. It is shaped like a black and white 8-ball. The questioner mentally asks his question, then inverts the 8-ball and an answer mystically appears.

The magic 8-ball was invented in 1946 by Abe Bookman. It consists of a hollow sphere containing a cylindrical chamber filled with a coloured dye and a dodecahedral or an icosahedral die floating in it. Each die face has an answer, that may be positive, negative or non-committal. It will float to the top to reveal the answer.

Figure 37: *The Magic 8-ball has a prediction screen opposite the 8, showing one of 20 answers supplied on the faces of the icosoheral dice within it.*

Destiny dice

Here you can use two dice of different colours, say a red die and a white die. The red die represents tens and the white single numbers. So that if a red six and a white one is thrown, then the questioner looks up the sixty-first answer.

This is more suited to general questions about the future, perhaps for a specific day, or a specific period.

11 – you are going to have to take a risk

12 – it is going to be hectic. Do be careful about your health

13 – there may be problems with a relationship

14 – be careful, someone may resent your success

15 – luck is with you

16 – a quarrel is possible

21 – your wish will be fruitful

22 – make sure all messages and correspondence have been taken care of

23 – good news is on its way

24 – it is not a good time to start something new

25 – an unexpected journey will have to be made

26 – a good time to enjoy the limelight

31 – not a time to gamble

32 – you must not be too trusting at this time

33 – it is a time to seek out old friends

34 – you may need to say sorry or be prepared to eat humble pie

35 – expect someone to interfere with your plans

36 – success is assured

41 – time to avoid unnecessary work

42 – there will be a delay, followed by a satisfactory outcome

43 – there may be a misunderstanding. Do not lose your temper

44 – now you need to get down to work. If you don't you will regret it

45 – love is in the air

46 – an old enemy is coming back on the scene

51 – bad luck prevails. Do not take chances

52 – you may get your wish if you are not too ambitious

53 – it is time to rest

54 – you have to be decisive

55 – you may lose something dear to you if you are not careful

56 – you need to be practical about things

61 – time to look after a friend or relative's needs rather than your own

62 – an unexpected windfall may occur soon

63 – study everything closely, especially any legal document or contract

64 – work to overcome a present difficulty and there will be success

65 – you need to be competitive to succeed

66 – expect unusual coincidences to occur

What the houses say

This is a simple style of casting that you can do with two small dice. It is, again, a general reading for a period ahead. The dice will indicate which areas of your life are most likely to be affected, according to where they land in the ring made up by your hands. The joints and joint spaces of your index fingers and thumbs will indicate the twelve astrological houses that are used in casting horoscopes.

Look at Figure 38 to get the idea. You cup the dice fully in your two hands and toss them about three times, then open the hands and gently toss the dice upwards, immediately bringing your hands down on the table; forming a ring with your index fingers and thumbs. Whichever of the two 'houses' that the dice land nearest to will indicate the areas of your life that are going to be of most relevance. The values of the dice will indicate what is liable to occur within those houses.

If both dice land outside your hands then try it once again. If they both land outside, then you are not being permitted to know this reading. If one lands outside on the second occasion, then it implies that there will be difficulty in whichever house that the die inside your circle is affected. The value on the die is irrelevant.

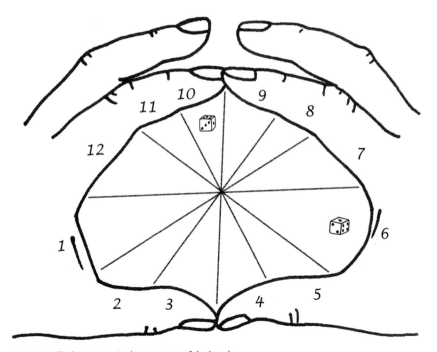

Figure 38: The houses are in the segments of the hands.

The Houses

First   – House of self – ego, first impressions, initiative
Second – House of value – money, stability, gifts
Third   – House of communication – letters, messages, books
Fourth – House of home and family
Fifth   – House of love and pleasure – relationships, leisure, amusement
Sixth   – House of health – general, hospitals, nutrition
Seventh – House of partnerships – colleagues, legal matters
Eighth   – House of the unknown – the occult, strange coincidences,
           luck
Ninth   – House of travel – journeys, foreign news
Ten   – House of social status – career, position, reputation
Eleven   – House of friends
Twelve – House of karma

The Numbers

1 – good luck
2 – negative vibes
3 – uncertainty
4 – there is activity underway, possibly expect a message to come
5 – a loss or reduction of some form is likely
6 – very positive outlook

It is emphasised that the methods outlined here are purely for fun. Do remember that you are a person who can make your own destiny. It is a risky business to rule your life by the dice or any other method of chance. Yet you may be the sort of person who would revel in such risk taking, like Luke Rhinehart, the eponymous antihero of the cult novel *The Dice Man*.

Chapter 10

Dice Control

First, I want to explain a little about this chapter, since dice control is a very grey area and I want to declare my position on the subject. I am neither a gambler nor a professional magician. I am an amateur conjurer with an interest in dice and the history of dice. In writing about dice control the main emphasis is on the game of craps, which is far more common in the USA than in Europe and the UK, although there are a few casinos here if one is keen to seek out action. The various techniques and moves that I am going to describe are used by people to gain an advantage in craps, but they can be used in a variety of the games that we will look at in the second section.

My purpose in including them in this book is also to warn you, so that you can detect if someone is gaining an unfair advantage. I regard their use in conjuring tricks as being a legitimate form of entertainment. When you read this chapter I am sure you will agree that some of the methods are nothing more than cheating, whereas others are skills that can be developed. The question is whether it is legitimate to use a skill to give an advantage in what should be a matter of chance is quite another matter.

I told you it was a grey matter.

What do we mean by control?

Most honest dice players 'will' the dice to turn up certain numbers. There is nothing wrong with that. But can it really be done?

A lot of serious gamblers who like to play with dice may think that they can influence the dice by some sort of power like psycho-kinesis (PK), also known as telekinesis. This is the ability to make something move through mind control. In fact this has been the subject of serious research by scientists for over the past eighty odd years. The first effective scientific research into psychic phenomena began in the 1920s, under the direction of Professor Joseph B. Rhine (1895–1980) in the psychology department at Duke University, North Carolina. This was to be the beginning of a new branch of psychology, called parapsychology.

Rhine's hypothesis was that if psychic abilities exist, then they should be apparent within the general population. Accordingly, his first subjects were recruited from the student body at Duke. He did this initially with the world famous Zener cards, which are used to test whether thoughts can be transferred from one person to another, or whether one can predict the order in which cards will fall. This was the basis of his early research on Extra Sensory Perception, or ESP. He published a book about it in 1934.

The study of telekinesis or the ability to make inanimate objects move was also tested by him in the late 1930s. To do this he first tested whether people could influence the roll of dice, first simply thrown by hand; then with dice thrown from a cup. Finally, to exclude any deliberate chicanery he used a dice-throwing machine.

I do not know of anyone who seriously believes that they can control the dice through the use of psycho-kinesis. I do have an open mind, however, and I am willing to be persuaded otherwise! Yet even if someone is able to control the dice in an experimental situation, I am doubtful whether it could be done in the course of a casino game like craps, or even with the simple roll of a die in a family game like Snakes and Ladders.

If you are of an experimental frame of mind then it is of course quite simple to see whether you are someone with the power of PK. I have shown you the different probabilities with one or two dice. All you need to do is show that you can throw the dice according to your predetermined values more frequently than simple chance.

If you can really do it, perhaps you had better book a flight to Las Vegas.

Physical dice control

Now this is a different matter. Dice tricksters have been using crooked dice for centuries. There are internet markets where you can purchase all manner of pre-arranged or doctored dice. Conjurers may use them to force a particular number on an unsuspecting spectator in the course of a magic trick. Unscrupulous people might use them to cheat at dice.

There are no bones about the use of crooked dice. It is simply dishonest and it is cheating.

Gambling games with dice have an element of skill, of course. For one thing you need to know what bets to make and which bets not to make. Understanding odds is a definite skill that will help you to maximise your chances of winning, or at least, reduce your chances of losing. Yet the question of whether you can actually control the dice is the real burning question that most aspiring crap-shooters want to know. Is it possible to deliberately throw any point, or avoid throwing a craps? And can it be done consistently better than probability would have you believe?

There is no doubt about it; it's big business in countries like the USA. People run classes, schools, shoot videos and write books on the subject. It is not something that can be learned overnight, they all will tell you, but if someone is diligent and willing to practice, then, yes, it can be learned.

Is it honest? Well that depends upon which side of the casino you are on. The casinos will all probably say that it is tantamount to cheating. Professional gamblers would probably say it is neither dishonest nor illegal, since you are not using crooked dice. Indeed, some would suggest that it is a way of evening up the edge that the house holds over each and every customer.

Dice control is considered akin to professional golf players being able to control a golf ball. That is, being able to hit a fade or a draw at will by putting spin on it.

Well, perhaps not exactly like that, because too much spin is precisely what you don't want!

Throw the dice or roll them

You will have heard both expressions. In craps you throw the dice or shoot them. In most family games you roll them.

Casino dice, as you know from Chapter 2 are precision made with straight faces and sharp edges. They will not tend to roll. They may bounce, but they will tend to turn just a few times.

In craps you throw or shoot the dice at a wall on the craps table so that they rebound. To make matters harder for anyone to control the dice the casinos also put small protuberances called 'pyramids' into the walls so that the dice will bounce off erratically thereby affecting any pre-arrangement of the dice.

In unofficial or private craps, that is, any craps game played outside a casino people tend to just play against a wall.

Professional crap-shooters would suggest that if someone is skilful he can do better than probability and, assuming that they know how to bet properly, can win more than they lose.

Ordinary shop or playing board game dice are not so precisely made and tend to have rounded or rolled edges, so they will assuredly roll. Indeed, in most friendly games the dice are just shaken then rolled from the hand. Yet there is still definitely scope to control them in these situations.

Dice cups

You would think that using a cup to shake the dice inside would remove all chance of control, wouldn't you? Well of course it does, as long as you are playing with honest folk. If you are playing a simple family game then it is highly likely that everyone is going to be playing honestly.

Once you introduce money into a game, then you are automatically gambling. If you are playing for small amounts then it is likely that you are just playing for fun. If the amounts are large, then can you trust that the other players are as honest as yourself?

If not, don't play.

The point is that using a cup actually gives anyone adept at sleight of hand a relatively easy opportunity to substitute crooked dice.

You may care to refresh your memory about the various types of crooked dice before playing for money with anyone that you do not know really well.

DICE CUP TIP

Always ensure that the dice are shaken so that they click and clack inside the cup. That means that they are rotated and will come out at random.

Dice cup control

Be aware that you can still be fooled! If dice are pre-arranged, and I will come to this in a moment, it is the very essence of dice control; there are a couple of ways of being deceived.

The Slide

The two dice are pre-arranged and slipped into the dice cup, or even scooped up. This is done slickly so that the dice do not turn over, but remain as a column of two (or however many are being used in the game) even when the cup is deftly tilted into the horizontal position.

Instead of shaking the cup, it is rotated round and round so that the column is swirled round by centrifugal force, so the dice will stay in a column on the side of the cup. When the player is ready to show the dice, instead of rolling them out, the dice cup is brought down into a horizontal position close to the table. It is given a slight jog forward and is then immediately retracted backwards, so that the dice slide out without rolling. There is a high likelihood that they will show the values he had pre-arranged.

Be watchful of someone using a slide to roll their dice. They have an edge on you.

The clip

This is a technique that may be used when multiple dice are loaded into the cup, as in poker dice. It is a means of controlling one die in order to give an edge.

The cup is generally held in the palm of the hand and, one-handed, the player scoops the dice into it with their fingers. The fingers are extended over the mouth of the cup like the flap of a pedal bin. The last die that was pre-arranged on the table, or pre-selected because it was showing the right value, (e.g. an ace in poker dice), is not flicked backwards into the cup but is clipped between the forefinger and second finger and held against the rim of the cup. The cup is then shaken, so that the other dice rattle.

The cup is deftly lowered to the table and the other dice are rolled out, whereas the clipped die is just placed on the table.

That may be all the edge that is needed in the game.

I emphasise that this is something to watch out for, it is not something to use in a game. It is a cheat's trick.

DICE CUP TIP

Do look to see what the dice cup is like. A shiny, smooth dice cup may have been chosen to facilitate 'the slide'.

If so, then make sure that you clarify at the start that the dice must be heard to rattle and that the dice must be expelled or rolled out rather than slid, before you start. If you do that then you will not be taken for someone who can be easily deceived.

The dice should be rattled not cackled

It is always a good idea to ask to hear the dice rattle, otherwise they may be deliberately pre-set. If people are not using a dice cup you should still be able to hear the dice being rattled.

A cackle is the name given to a false rattle. The dice are picked up by the first three fingers and the thumb in what I describe as the 'cackle hold'. It is also

Figure 39: The Cackle or Lock grip.

known as the '*lock grip*'. The last joint of the thumb is flexed, so that the dice rest against the nail and the three fingers effectively form a cage around the two dice. If they have been pre-set (and we look at this later) then an up and down movement of the hand will allow the dice to move against one another, or cackle. It sounds as though they are being rattled and randomly turned, but the pre-set arrangement has been maintained.

THROWING TECHNIQUES

If you are playing in a private gambling game with dice, then you should be aware of house rules. The same really goes for ordinary board games. In other words, make absolutely certain that there is a rule about how the dice can be played. If you are not playing on a firm table, but are using a carpet or bed, or blanket, then it is certainly possible to control the dice to some extent.

Now let us look at rolling and throwing techniques.

Rolling the dice

In lots of games it is permitted to roll the dice. If they are properly shaken and rattled prior to a proper roll, then the result should be entirely random. That is fair.

The following methods may give someone an edge. Once again, the purpose of this section is only to show you how to detect when someone is trying to control dice in a game.

Sleight of hand

There are various methods or sleights by which conjurers conceal objects such as dice in their hands. The basic method is called 'palming'. This means that a die is held concealed in the palm of the hand, or clipped between fingers in a 'finger palm'. As I mentioned at the start of the chapter this is legitimate in a magic trick, but is reprehensible in a game. It is cheating. I do not propose to explain the techniques, but merely warn you to watch closely the hands of a player in a game if you are playing for any gain.

Blanket roll

This is the name given to a simple method of rolling the dice in an informal setting outside a casino. It is also called the 'pad roll' or the 'soft roll'. The dice are preset and held in the caged position of the 'cackle hold' that I described when performing the cackle or false rattle. It is an easy matter then to roll the dice from the hand so that the two dice simply rotate about the horizontal axis (a line drawn through the centre of both dice from left to right) once or twice. Pre-set dice will eliminate two faces from each die, so the odds of rolling certain numbers will be changed, and probably not to the advantage of anyone but the dice roller.

Key point

In any board game played with one die, if the aim is to avoid a certain number of squares from one to six, then if the die is orientated with the number at one side and a blanket roll given, then the odds are shortened markedly.

If you don't want this to happen then use a dice cup, even with one die.

The whip shot

The dice are again picked up in a pre-set fashion (the top face of each die are the ones desired to show face up) as in the cackle grip and a cackle is done to convince everyone that a rattle has been made. Then the thumb is moved slightly forward so that the dice are held against the second, third and fourth fingers. The hand is brought down to touch the table and the wrist is quickly flexed like a whip and the thumb imparts a spin to them. This will cause the dice to spin clockwise. They will land like spinning tops but will not actually roll. They will land together with the desired faces showing upwards.

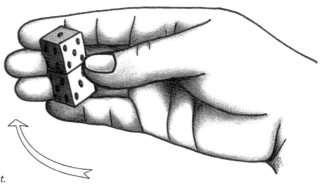

Figure 40: The whip shot.

Rhythm rolling

This is the name given to the technique of being able to reproduce exactly the same rhythm each time. It is a repeatable throw that will produce a repeatable roll of the pre-set dice, moving only on their horizontal axis so that they will tend to give the desired numbers.

It is certainly something that one can practice for board games. Just knowing how far the dice will roll will increase the number of occasions your favoured numbers will come up.

Get a golf ball or other small ball and just practice doing a blanket roll on a carpet or covered table. Aim at being able to roll it a set distance so that you can repeatedly do that. Then try doing the same with one die. When you feel you can do that with your blanket roll, try doing it with two.

Throwing dice

Casinos insist that the shooter throws or shoots the dice the length of the craps table. The dice have to hit the back wall and bounce off. It is clearly going to be very difficult to control dice in such circumstances, yet it may be possible to shorten the odds. People do this by pre-arrangement and by the use of a variety of throwing techniques.

If you throw and bounce the dice off the table before they hit the back wall they will almost certainly end up as a random throw. For this reason most shooters will try to hit the back wall with just enough force so that they bounce off and roll a minimum number of times. Controlled dice will have been put in a pre-set fashion, which we come to soon.

Over the years, much of the literature about dice control relates to how players can get an edge in the game of craps, and a lot of the terminology relates to this.

In craps two dice are thrown at a time. There is little point in throwing dice with the greatest of skill if you have no idea of what you are hoping the dice will do. Essentially, if you start with both dice in one position the aim of the throw is to get them to land so that the faces showing relate to the initial set up. The throw should result in minimum alteration of the faces once they land. I will come to this pre-arrangement shortly.

Let me begin by talking about the game of golf. Although there are not obvious similarities there is a principle that is important: that is, the nature of spin.

In golf a ball is struck in a set way with a particular club that is designed for different shots. Basically in each shot the ball is struck so that it goes off at the desired trajectory, flies through the air in a predictable manner and then lands and rolls according to the type of shot that was made. The purpose of a drive is to hit it long and straight with top spin, so that when it hits the ground the top spin will tend to keep it rolling forward so that it goes the maximum distance. When you get closer to the green, you choose clubs with increasing amount of loft so that they will tend to produce more and more backspin. Thus, a pitch shot to the green will cause a high ball that will drop to the green with backspin that will limit the mount of further forward movement. The ideally struck pitch shot should land and stop within a few inches or land and roll backwards.

You cannot, of course, expect a die to have the same flight characteristics as a sphere. It is a cube and it does not roll like a round object. If you just toss a die and watch it fall it will bounce and roll quite erratically, depending upon whether it lands on a face, edge or corner. Most people will in fact toss it totally randomly so that its eventual result will be a simple matter of chance.

Someone aiming at dice control will try to reduce its erratic roll, possibly by trying to impart backspin. It is a knack that people are often willing to pay a lot of money to learn.

Understand the basics

You might find it useful to get a pair of casino dice and a pair of shop dice and toss them about. See the way that they fall and bounce and roll. Casino dice, which have sharper edges on them, will not actually roll in the way that the curved edges of shop dice will do.

If you now pick up a pair of dice (either your casino or the shop dice) and toss them forward, as you tend to do when you roll them in a board game, you will probably see that they land, bounce and separate. One will bounce in one direction while the other may go off in another direction. Or they can hop in one direction and then another until they eventually use up all of their energy and settle. And you know from the previous chapter on Odds and Probability that how they land will be a mater of pure chance.

Key point

There is no predictability about how a pair of randomly thrown dice will land. There are probabilities and odds, but there is no predictability.

Orientate the die

If you have a die in front of you get used to thinking of its faces like this: top, back (towards you), bottom, front, then left side, and right side.

The corners are always the problem with thrown dice. When a die lands on a corner it will bounce sideways. A die landing on a right corner will bounce and roll to the left and a die landing on a left corner will bounce and roll to the right. Experiment with this and get to understand the manner of these erratic bounces.

If two dice land and bounce so that they cross over it means that they have separated and were already rotating.

A double pitch
A die landing on an edge will roll in the direction of that edge. If one die of a pair lands on a face it will bounce, but not with the speed of one landing on an edge. This means that the faster die will rotate its face at least one, and probably two or more than the other. Double pitches are not what you want to throw in craps, unless you have pre-set to a particular combination and are aiming for a seven. I will explain when I talk about pre-arrangements.

Key point
A controlled dice throw aims to get both dice moving through the air and behaving in the same way.

The axes of rotation
Look at Figure 41. There are three axes through the centres of two dice, as they start off together. The horizontal axis from left to right, the vertical axis through the bottom and top, and the back to front axis.

The important thing in throwing the dice is to aim at maintaining the horizontal axis. If you can eliminate or reduce bouncing to left or right then you reduce the chances of randomisation. A bounce and roll in dice in the horizontal axis will tend to make the dice either land on one of the pairs of faces that were originally set or you will get them out of phase. If one has rolled two or more from its original place then that is called a double pitch.

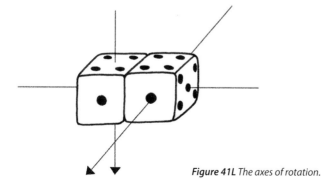

Figure 41L *The axes of rotation.*

Different grips

As long as you propel the dice forward with a toss, so that they are airborne and they travel through the air, then that is a dice throw. As mentioned above, in lots of games you will be expected to use a dice cup. In board games you probably use your cupped hands, or you throw them. In craps you throw them the length of the table and they have to bounce off the back wall.

Casinos prefer to see the dice held in the hand and like to hear them rattle. Yet you can grip them how you like as long as you throw.

The three-fingered front grip

Many crap-shooters use this grip, which is a bit like lifting sugar cubes. Imagine that you were lifting two dice from the top of a sugar bowl with your fingers. Three fingers at the front of the two dice and the thumb at the rear. The thumb holds the two dice at the point of contact. That is all it does, it does not launch them. The forward motion of the hand imparts the necessary momentum. The dice will fly with some backspin.

If you flick the thumb forward to help them on their way you will cause them to drift apart and they will land independently and bounce erratically to give a random result.

It is frequently used because it gives you the ability to get the die moving forward together in the air in the right plane.

The 'blanket roll' and the 'lock grip' are the two other most used grips in craps. These are underarm throws, so obviously they are not going to impart backspin. The shooter is going to try to develop rhythm rolling, so that they are able to produce a controlled flight, bounce and roll.

Whatever grip is used the ultimate aim is to maintain the dice through the air in the horizontal plane so that after hitting the back wall, there will be minimal movement of the paired faces.

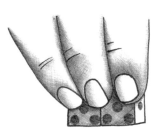

Figure 42: The 3-fingered front grip.

Dice setting

Undoubtedly setting the dice in a certain position before rolling them in board and casual games will improve the chances of throwing whatever sum you need.

You may think that if you set the dice with the desired numbers facing upwards, then rhythm rolling is all that there is to it. This is not so. The most important faces are the ones that face each other.

Get a pair of dice and check out all of this.

The point is that if you roll dice you cannot be sure whether they will roll together or roll erratically. True you are minimising it by using some of the techniques I have discussed, yet one die may roll more than the other to mix things up. But, if you have removed the values of the outer two faces and the two faces that touch, then you have effectively taken them out of the equation. It is simple mathematics. All you have to aim at is to keep them rolling forward and maintaining the horizontal axis so that they do not rotate sideways.

Simple mathematics

If you put a six **or** one and six **or** one facing each other and roll them, you cannot make a two, three, eleven, or twelve. In the game of craps that means you can't make a craps. You also reduce your chance of rolling a seven, which would mean you lost if you were going for a point (see the game of craps in section 2).

If you need a four, then put six **or** one, and four **or** three facing. This will increase your chances of rolling it. Again, you reduce your chances of making seven

If you need a five or nine, or a six or eight, then put six **or** one and five **or** two together. This will increase your chances of rolling any of them. Again, you reduce your chances of making seven.

The Flying 3-V set up

If you need to avoid a seven, which you need to do in craps after the roll out, then the *Flying V set up* takes a seven out of the equation.

Set a six **or** one facing a five **or** two. Then look at the uppermost faces. Rotate the threes so that they are together. They will produce the Flying V. Experiment and you will find that the threes produce either a 'V' or an inverted 'V'.

With a blanket roll you will not roll a seven.

Figure 43: *the Flying 3-V set up.*

Figure 44: the 2-V set up.

The 2-V set up
If you set the twos into Vs, with six **or** one facing four **or** three, then you have a good chance of rolling a four or ten.

Doubles
If you are aiming for doubles, then align them up straight, so that the sixes are like tram lines, with three **or** four facing three **or** four.

Part 2

Dice Games

STANDARD DICE NOTATION
This indicates the type of dice needed in any game. The small letter 'd' is used to designate 'die' or 'dice'. This is followed by the number of faces, e.g. d6 indicates a six-sided dice. A numeral preceding the d is used to indicate the number of dice needed in any game, e.g. 2d6 means that two six-sided dice are needed. I will be using this notation throughout this games section.

START WITH A HIGH ROLL
This is the term for choosing the first person to play. Basically, each person rolls a die and the high score gets to play first.

Chapter 11

Knucklebones (Jacks)

The precursors of dice were called knucklebones. It seems entirely appropriate to start this section on dice games by looking at how you can play this most ancient of games.

As we saw in Chapter 2 these were made from the ankle bones of hoofed animals, like sheep, goats and oxen. The specific bone is the talus, otherwise known as the astragalus. Thus they became known by the Greeks and Romans as *astralgi* or 'knucklebones'.

A knucklebone is basically tetrahedral in shape, so that it can land in one of four positions. Each face is distinguishable from the others. One face is concave, one is convex, the third is almost flat and the fourth is slightly undulating.

There are various games that are played with knucklebones, which are known by different names. Jacks, Jackstones, Fivestones, Chuckstones and Hucklebones are examples. People even play with small stones or chips which have multiple faces like knucklebones.

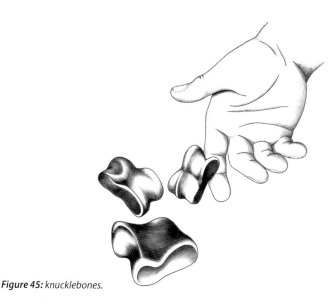

Figure 45: knucklebones.

You can buy a set of knucklebones from most dice suppliers. Some are made of metal and others are made of synthetic materials. It is not considered hygienic to use actual bone these days, but if you are determined you will be able to obtain a set from collectors' fairs or from the Internet.

A little history

Museums and art galleries around the world have knucklebones sets and depictions of knucklebones being played by gods, goddesses and ordinary mortals. The British Museum has a beautiful little terracotta piece with two figurines of ancient Greek women playing knucklebones. The Museum of Naples has a painting that was excavated from Pompeii, showing the goddesses Latona, Niobe, Phoebe, Aglaia and Hileaera, the latter two playing happily with the bones.

Although they would undoubtedly have been used for divinatory purposes, their erratic way of bouncing would have made them quite suited to gambling. Many cultures fostered that use but others outlawed it. Nevertheless, games were developed with them, not all of them depending upon the numeric values that one could ascribe to the different faces. Indeed, in the games that have come down to us it seems that knucklebones tended to be used for amusement, as games of dexterity and skill.

How to play knucklebones

Requirements
Either obtain an actual set of knucklebones or use five small pebbles or sea shells.

Number of players
One or as many as desired

Aim of the game
First to complete a series of set tasks. You select which tasks you want to do (from the selection of throws given below) and the order in which they should be done. Each person gets a turn and goes through as many of the throws as they can until they fail, then it is the turn of the person next to them on their left. You go round the circle until you are back to the first person again. Each person has to complete their throw before they are able to move to the next level.

Generally start with the youngest person or with a female if playing in mixed company.

THE THROWS

These are great fun. You go through a series of one, twos, threes and fours. But first you have to do the basic throw. This is sometimes called 'jockeying'.

Gather all five knucklebones or stones in the cupped hand. Then toss them up in the air and quickly turn your hand over and try to catch as many stones as you can on the back of the hand. You can spread your fingers to give a larger landing surface. Any that fall off are left on the ground or table.

Then reverse this throw, so that you flick the knucklebones from the back of the hand into the air, and then catch them in your hand. Any that you drop you leave on the surface. Of the ones that you catch you select one and put the others aside. The one you select is your '*sky bone*' or '*sky stone*'. It is the one that you are going to repeatedly throw.

The more that you have been able to put aside the better, since you will have less to do on the throws.

Sweeps

Ones

You start with 'ones'. You throw the sky bone into the air and while it is still in the air you scoop up one of the bones on the ground (of the ones you had previously failed to catch). You must catch the sky bone and not let it drop.

Each bone that you manage to pick up you put aside with the others. You keep doing it until you have picked up each of the remaining bones one at a time.

If the sky bone touches the surface your throw is over. If you had not completed the ones then you have to retry when it is your turn again.

If you completed ones, you go onto twos.

Twos

You start again with five bones and do the basic toss, putting any that you manage to catch aside. Choose your sky bone again.

This time you have to pick up two bones at a time. If the bones on the surface have scattered, then you are allowed to sweep them closer while you throw the sky bone. When they are close enough you have to pick two up at once. If there was only one bone on the surface then you just scoop it up; as long as the sky bone does not drop.

Threes

You guessed it, you have to pick up three at a time.

Fours
And then four.

Scatters
These are also done in ones, twos, threes, and fours. To begin with you scatter the bones on the table or ground. Select a sky bone and as with sweeps you have to pick up ones, then twos, then threes. It can be very hard to pick up all three bones at once without dropping the sky bone.

You are not permitted to sweep with scatters.

Juggles
This is really fun and as with any type of juggling activity is good for hand eye coordination.

Staring with all five bones on the ground select one as the sky bone. Toss it up in the air and while it is up toss another into the air. Catch the sky bone, then catch the other. Repeat this one at a time until you have caught them all in your hand.

Over the line
Here you do a basic throw and select your sky bone. Then place your other hand flat on the ground, as the line. Any bones that you had successfully caught you place on the other side of the line out of the way. Then toss the sky bone up and while it is in the air you pick up a bone and place it over the line with the others. Repeat until they are all over the line and then remove your hand. Throw the sky bone and scoop up all the bones in one hand.

Into the cup
This is also fun. Choose your sky bone. Then with your free hand lightly make a fist so that your thumb and first finger are touching to make a circle. Place this fist on the ground so that it is like a cup.

Then just as in scatter ones throw up the sky bone and while it is in the air pick up a bone and drop it into the cup. Do this until all four have been deposited down the hole.

Air bones
This is exactly the same as 'Into the Cup' except this time you hold the 'cup' in the air at chest height. The bones are dropped through the hole so they are air bones!

Stable the horses

Here you make a set of four stables with your free hand. Do this by spreading the thumb and fingers and resting the tips on the floor so that your four stables have open doors.

Scatter the bones as usual and select a sky bone; then throwing it in the air, one by one flick or sweep a bone or 'horse' into a stable. Each of the four bones must go into a separate stable. Once all four have been stabled, then lift the hand and throw the sky bone up and scoop up all four horses.

Witch's teeth

Put a bone in between finger and thumb and between the other fingers of the free hand, so that these represent the troublesome teeth. Lay the hand on the ground and toss the sky bone in the air. While it is airborne pull one of the witch's teeth then catch the sky bone. Toss it again and lay the tooth down beside the hand. Keep repeating until the witch's teeth have all been pulled. Finally, toss the sky bone up again and pick up all the teeth and catch the sky bone.

Chapter 12

Medieval Games

In Flanders whilom was a company
Of younge folkes, that haunted folly,
As riot, hazard, stewes, and taverns;
Where as with lutes, harpes, and giterns,
They dance and play at dice both day and night,

The Pardoner's Tale from *The Canterbury Tales*
Geoffrey Chaucer

As we saw at the start of the book, dice as we now know them have been used since antiquity. The Serpent game, the Royal Game of Ur and Senet were all played in the cradle lands of civilisation. Their rules have been lost in the mists of time and the best that we can do is speculate about the way that they were played.

Other board games, that are possibly almost as old, are still played in various parts of the world and some have even been resurrected, and sold commercially today. That is quite fascinating since it shows both how sophisticated our ancestors were, and yet how easily we can relinquish our computers and game consoles and still be amused by those simple games from the past. The dice still hold their ability to amuse us.

In the last chapter we looked at the oldest of games played with the precursors of dice, knucklebones, now I shall look at a few of the games that were played in medieval times and which thrive today in relatively undiluted forms. And we shall see how the simple game of Hazard that was played by Crusaders evolved into one of the most popular gambling games in the world, played in the glitziest of Las Vegas casinos as well as in downtown alleys across the world.

FARKLE

(Played with 6d6 = 6 normal dice)
This game is centuries old. How many is not quite clear, since there are several ideas about its origin. One is that a Sir Albert Farkle played it in 1492 in Iceland.

Another source maintains that it was played on French sailing ships. A variant of it is covered by a trademark as Farkel, manufactured by Legendary Games.

It has various names and you may know it as 5,000, 10,000, Zilch, Kaput, or Dix Mille in France. It can also be played with five dice as Cosmic Wimpout, or Keepers.

It is a scoring game that can be played by two or more people. It is a great family game and also a game popular with students who play it as a forfeit game. It is certainly a game of skill if you understand odds, as I hope you do from reading the earlier chapters.

How to play Farkle

There is a particular scoring system in Farkle. The aim is to reach a score of 5,000. It is taken in turns to play and each player rolls the dice until he either makes a score and banks, or they fail and farkle. A farkle means no score; you lose even the points you had rolled in that turn before you 'farkled'.

You have to score 500 points on one turn to get on the board, and after that you have to score a minimum of 350.

The scoring is as follows:

Each 1 = 100
Each 5 = 50

In addition:

3 × 1 = 1,000 points
3 × 2 = 200
3 × 3 = 300
3 × 4 = 400
3 × 5 = 500
3 × 6 = 600

(in other words, it is the number of the triple multiplied by 100)

Or

3 pairs on one roll = 750

Or

A straight 1, 2, 3, 4, 5, 6 on one roll would make either 1,500 or 2,000, whichever you decide at the start of the game.)

To start play a 'High Roll' is used to determine who plays first. Each person rolls a die and the high score gets to play first. Having then decided on the starting player, he rolls all six dice and moves to the side all scoring dice. At least one scoring dice must be placed aside on each roll. For example, if you roll three ones, a three, two and six, you score 1,000.

You then have the option of banking, so you let the next player go, or you can opt to increase your score with the three non-scoring dice. That would probably not be a good move, because if you farkle and have no scoring dice in that roll you lose the 1,000 points. It would be a gamble.

If all six dice score them you can roll all six again, but of course, it is a gamble. It depends how the game is going whether you should do that, which is what makes it fun.

Variations
- You can have 5,000 or 10,000 as the line that you have to cross, or you can make it an exact target.
- Some people prefer to use five dice and play to 5,000, or six dice and 10,000
- You can include 'piggybacking'. This means that if one player banks, you can piggyback by deciding to roll the non-scoring dice. If you score then you get the banked score plus the new score. The previous player keeps his score of course.
- If a player farkles three times in a row they have 1,000 or 2,000 points deducted.

GLUCKHAUS

(Played with 2d6 = two normal dice)
This is another very old game that dates back to the Sixteenth Century. It is German in origin and means 'House of Fortune'. It is played on a board or a scratched grid with eleven numbers on it.

Two dice are used and you can have two or as many players as you wish. It is a good game for children. You can play it with money, matches, counters or chocolate buttons. Roll a die to see who starts. Highest die begins.

There is no number four.
Number 2 is the lucky pig
Number 7 is the wedding invitation
Number 12 is the King

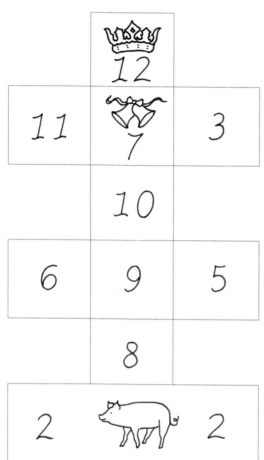

Figure 46: *Gluckhaus the House of Fortune.*

How to play Gluckhaus

The first player rolls both dice and places a coin or whatever type of counter is being used on the square of that value. The next player does the same.

If a coin is already on the square then the player picks that up. If it is empty he puts one down. The seven is for wedding gifts so you always add coins to it, until it is cleared.

A two is the lucky pig and when this is thrown all the coins are picked up except for the wedding square, which can accumulate a stack.

A 12 is the king and he takes everything, including the wedding gifts in taxes.

A four misses a turn and neither gains nor loses a coin.

There is only an end to the game when you decide to stop.

HAZARD

(Played with 2d6 = 2 normal dice)
As indicated at the start of this chapter, the game of Hazard was played back in the Thirteenth Century, during the days of Geoffrey Chaucer. It is thought to be even older than that and may have been played by bored crusaders during the lengthy siege of an Arabian castle, called Hazarth or Asart in 1125. Sir William of Tyre is reputed to have invented it and the name of Hazard is a corruption of the castle's name.

It was popular in medieval times and became hugely popular in the Seventeenth and Eighteenth Centuries. As we shall see in the next chapter, it evolved into one of the most popular casino games in America.

It is a gambling game played with two dice and two or any number of players.

Dice control

Please note that all of the information in the chapter on Dice Control is relevant to Hazard.

Playing with a dice cup is sensible, but also be sure to have considered the section on dice control with a dice cup.

How to play Hazard
This is quite complex since the rules change within the game.

As is common, everyone rolls one die to determine who starts. The thrower is called *the 'caster'*.

The caster begins by placing his bet in the centre of the playing area. The *'setters'*, as the other players are called place their bets in the area as well. When the caster accepts the bets he knocks the table.

If the caster wins at the end of a game he takes all the money. If he loses, then the setters take their stakes back and an equal share of the caster's stake.

The caster keeps throwing until he loses three times, then the person to his left becomes the caster.

On the opening throw the caster is trying to score a main point. This has to be a number between five and nine, inclusive. If he does not make such a total then he continues throwing until he does. That number is then considered the *'main point'*.

He then throws again.

The same number wins

- If the main point is a six or eight and a 12 is rolled, he wins
- If the main point is a seven and an 11 is rolled, he wins. This is called *a 'nick'*.
- If a four, five, six, seven, eight, nine or 10 is thrown then this is called a *'chance point'*, as long as it is not the same number as the main point.
- Here the rule changes – with the next roll he wins if he throws the same as the chance number, but loses if he rolls the main number. He continues until one of these numbers is rolled.
- If he rolls an *'out'* he loses. An out is a two or a three, which is called *a 'crab'*, or a 12 when the main point is a five, six, eight or nine.

I told you it was complex.

MIA

(Played with 2d6 = 2 normal dice)
This is an old Viking game of bluff. You need to have a knowledge of odds and what makes a good hand.

It is also virtually identical to Liar dice, which has become famous in the UK as a result of the film *Pirates of the Caribbean*.

For this you need two dice and a flat bottomed dice container with a lid. It can be played by three or more players. Each player has a number of lives, say three, but you decide how many depending on how long you want to play.

How to play Mia
The first player shakes the dice and then checks the result. He then has three choices:

- He can tell the truth
- He can lie and say that he has more than he has
- He can lie and say he has less than he has

He then slides the pot to the next player, who does not remove the lid. He can either:
Accept the first player as telling the truth and then he shakes to try to beat the first player

He calls the first player a liar and checks to see. If the result is lower than the first player claimed, then the first player loses a life. If the result is true or higher than he said, then the current player loses a life.

Accepts that the first player was telling the truth and he passes it on to the next player. The first player is out of danger and the player who passes is now at risk if he is challenged and the result is less than stated.

There is a set way of scoring. It is not an addition, but a way of making one die stand for tens and the other for units. The higher of the two is always the tens.

A score of 21 is called Mia and is the highest score, which cannot be beaten.
Then the doubles come next, starting with ones. So the order is 11, 22, 33, 44, 55, 66.
Then the numbers reduce, thus 65, 64, 63, 62, 54, 53, 52, 51, 43, 42, 41, 32.
Thus the sequence from highest hand to lowest is:
21, 11, 22, 33, 44, 55, 66, 65, 64, 63, 62, 61, 54, 53, 52, 51, 43, 42, 41, 32.

If a player loses a life then the pot returns to the player before, who rolls again and a new game starts.

Each player must declare that a higher number than the person before, or they pass, or they call the previous player a liar.

If the dice come back to the original player he must declare a higher number. He cannot pass it.

If the dice pot has returned to the original player and he had actually thrown a Mia, then he can roll the dice again and start another game.

If Mia is announced then the player at risk of losing a life loses two lives

COCKFIGHTING

(Played with 6d6 = 6 normal dice)
This is an old Chinese gambling game. It is also called Ta Ki.
One player is the banker. The other players place bets.

How to play Cockfighting
The banker rolls all six dice and depending on the scores, he will win and bank their stakes, let it ride or lose and pay out.

The different scores pay out different amounts.

Bank wins

Six of a kind	player pays 7:1
Five of a kind	player pays 7:1
High pairs fours, fives, sixes	player pays 7:1

Four of a kind with the remaining two dice adding up to the value of the four. Thus, three and three to make six, and three and two to make five, etc. the player would pay 3:1

Three of a kind with the remaining three dice totalling five or 14 and over. The player would pay 1:1

Bank loses

Low pairs ones, twos, threes. Banks pays 7:1

Three of a kind with the remaining three dice totalling, four, six or seven. Bank pays 1:1

Chapter 13

Craps

(Played with 2d6 = two normal dice)

The game of craps is derived from Hazard, which we looked at in the last chapter. It is thought that Hazard was introduced to the Americas by the English settlers who sailed there on the *Mayflower*. It gradually evolved into the game now known as craps.

It is thought that the name is derived from a corrupted version of *the 'crab'*, the throw of a two or three in the chance throw of Hazard. Another version is that it referred to the toad-like position that people get into as they hunch over the table. The French word *crapaud* was then abbreviated to craps.

The game of craps is supposedly simpler than Hazard, although a look at any casino craps table may convince you otherwise. It was certainly played extensively on the Mississippi riverboats. It has had an altogether chequered history and has been played in alleys, back streets, in private games, and in casinos. The incredibly successful musical *Guys and Dolls* revolves around a floating craps game. This meant that it was a game that floated, or was moved from place to place, since it was illegal to play it. The term was introduced by Damon Runyon, a journalist and writer who specialised in stories of the Prohibition era.

If you are going to play craps in a private game, then note the information about crooked dice. If you play in a casino, then the dice will be transparent, precision made and will only be in the game for a few hours. Casino dice should be safe.

Internet casinos offer an altogether different form of craps. This is virtual craps, played with computer-generated dice. Obviously a player has no control over such a game and there is plenty of scope to lose a lot of money. Although they are regulated so that there is no danger of a game being fixed it is easy to become hooked on such games. Be very careful, is my advice.

A game of skill?

Undoubtedly craps is a very skilful game. It is not a game to just venture into without having knowledge of the rules. It is also important to understand the various types of bet and the odds on various numbers. I have covered odds in an earlier chapter and you should read and assimilate the information therein before ever venturing near a craps table.

Very importantly, there are certain bets that you should simply not make in craps and we shall look at some of these. Otherwise you may be betting at less than straightforward chance.

Bank craps

In the Nineteenth Century John H. Winn, a dice-maker introduced a grid that changed the rules of craps so that a better can bet for or against the shooter. This largely resulted in crooked dice being useless and led to the development of the modern game played in casinos around the world. He is considered to be the father of modern craps.

Yet be warned, there are outlets on the Internet where one can obtain crooked dice and they might be used in private games. I emphasise again, be very sure of the dice if invited to such a game.

Bank craps is the type of game played in the casinos. It is usually the noisy, exciting part of a casino. There will be a lot of congratulating, high-fiving and an equal amount of commiserating going on.

A craps table is about the same size as a pool table. It has a tightly stretched green baize on it with a complicated looking grid printed with various numbers. These relate to the different bets.

There is a rail all round the table. There is a groove outside it for players to place their chips, which you should buy from the cashier when you enter the casino. Under that is usually a shelf for drinks.

A craps table has to have a 'crew' of people operating it. This consists of a boxman, a stickman, two dealers and a pit boss. The pit boss will be looking after several craps tables.

The boxman sits in the middle of the table and supervises the game. He makes sure that there is no cheating, that none of the chips on the table are moved and that all payments are made.

The stickman stands opposite the boxman. He will call out numbers thrown. He has a hooked stick which he uses to move the dice to the shooter. He also moves a craps marker puck onto a box number when a point has been made. When a game is in play this will be turned one side up to indicate this, and when the game is over he will turn it to show black.

The two dealers stand on either side of the boxman and deal with bets on their ends of the table.

As mentioned in the chapter on dice control, tables have small protruding pyramids or bumps at the end of the table in order to make the dice fly off erratically.

How to play craps

Craps is a betting game in which players bet on the outcome of a pair of thrown dice.

The player throwing the dice is called *the 'shooter'*. He throws the dice at the other end of the table, aiming to make the dice hit the wall and then stop quickly. They do have to hit the ball wall however or it is *'no dice'*. This means that the throw does not count and has to be made again. If only one dice rebounds then the dice throw is counted, but the other players may complain. Remember that they may be betting against the shooter.

- The shooter places his bet.
- The other players make their bets.
- The shooter's first throw is called the *'come out throw'*. If he throws a seven or an 11, this is called a natural. He immediately wins. So too will players betting for him.
- If his come out is a two, three or 12, it is called craps, and he loses.
- Any other number is called *'the point'*.
- He continues to throw until he either throws a seven, which is called 'seven *out'*, in which case he loses, or he throws the point, which is called *'making the point'*, then he wins.
- A shooter's win is called a *'pass'*.
- A shooter's loss is called a *'miss'*.
- The shooter keeps playing for as long as he is winning. When he loses by seven outing, he passes the dice to the player on his left.
- A player may choose not to play and simply pass the dice to the next player on his left.
- That is the essence of the game.

Betting at craps

Betting is what it is all about, however. To understand it a little better take a look at Figure 47, which shows the right half of a craps table.

Notice the following areas:

Pass line – a bet placed here means that you are backing the shooter to make a seven or 11 on his come out throw, or to make his point on the next throw. This is the commonest bet.

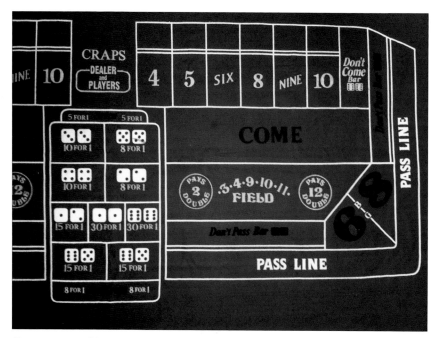

Figure 47: craps table.

Don't pass line – a bet here means that you are betting against the shooter, so that if he throws a two or three, a crap, he loses, but you win. Note that on this line it also says 'bars 66'. This means that if he throws a double six, making 12, although he will have lost, it is not decided for the 'don't pass' betters. They have the option of either leaving it there for the next throw or they can take it back. The reason is to give the casino a slight edge. In some casinos it may be 11 instead of a double six.

If the shooter throws a natural on his come out, he wins and you lose.

[N.B. A wrong better is someone who bets that the shooter will lose.]

Come line – this is used for placing a bet after the come out throw and the point has been made. You will win if the shooter throws a seven or 11 and you lose if he throws two, three or 12. If another number is made then the bet is moved to that number and it stays there until either the shooter makes the point or he 'seven outs'.

Don't come line – this is the small box beside the number 10. It is the reverse of a come bet. It can be placed any time after the come out throw. You win if a two or three is thrown, but a 12 is barred, so you can either take it away or leave it. If a seven or 11 comes up you lose.

Any other number becomes the point and the bet is placed in the box. If a seven comes up before the point, you win. If the point comes up before a seven you lose.

Field – this is for a bet that can be made at any stage. It is a single roll bet. If the shooter on the next throw makes three, four, nine, 10 or 11, then you win even money. If he throws two you win 2:1. Some casinos also pay double if you hit 12, but it will be shown if they do. Any other number you lose.

Hardway bets – these are found in the middle of the table. There are four hardway boxes with dice pictures in them. The dealer places them for you.

There are four hardways, meaning four totals that must be made one way only. They are hardway six made by two threes; hardway eight made by two fours; hardway 10 made by two fives and hardway four made by two twos.

To win a hardway bet your hardway must come up before a seven.

These usually pay well, but they vary casino by casino.

Hardway four or 10 pays 6 or 7 to 1

Hardway six or eight pays 8 or 9 to 1.

If you look at the chapter on odds, you will see that the chances of making a seven are considerably more than making any hardway.

Any seven – just above the hardways bets you can place an 'any seven' bet. This is a single roll bet and it is for a seven. If the shooter seven outs on the next roll you win 5:1. This is not a bad bet, because as you know there are six ways to make a seven.

Single bets

Underneath the hardway bet boxes there are five single roll bets. A bet in one of these is determined by the next roll. They may look tempting, but consider the odds. Check up on them in Figure 47.

It should be quite clear that these are not easy to make and even although they pay out well, you may have to place a lot of bets to recoup with these big paybacks.

Aces or snake eyes – a double one on this throw pays out 30:1.
Twelve craps or **Boxcars** – a double six on this throw pays out 30:1.
Eleven *or* **Six-Five** – if an 11 is thrown then you win 15:1

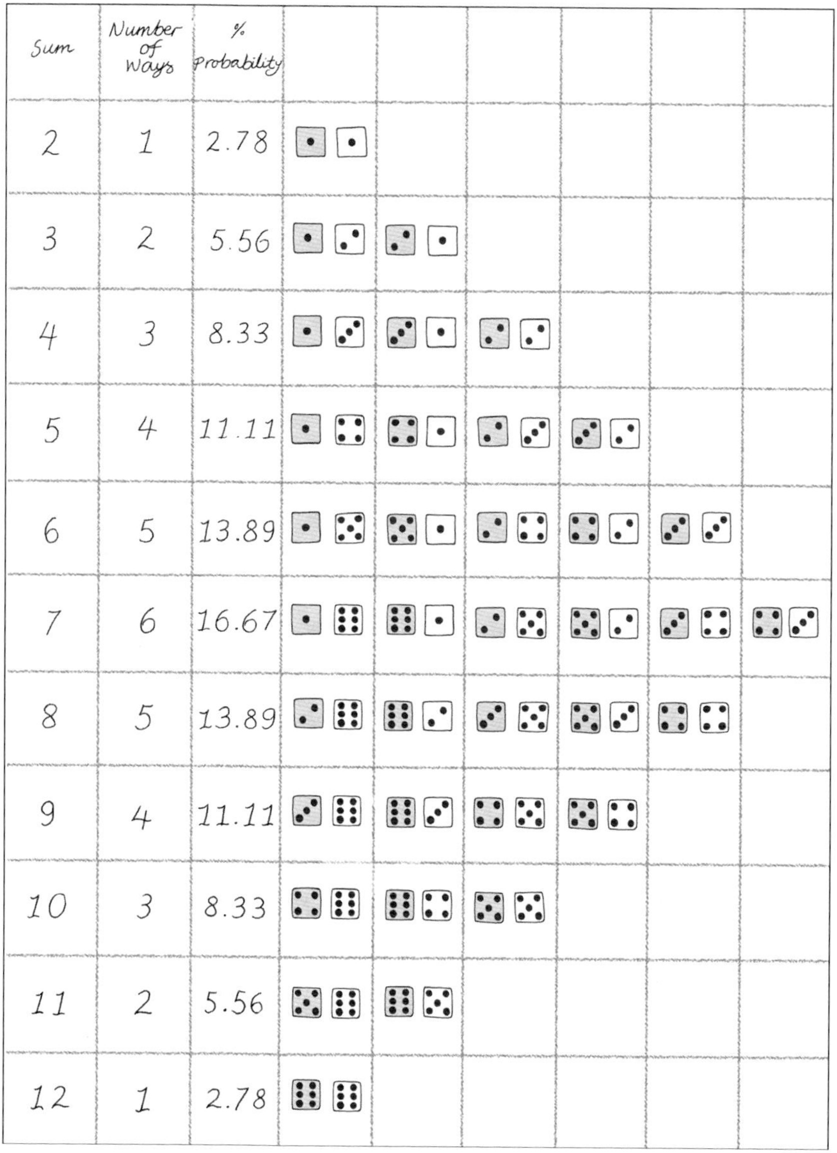

Sum	Number of Ways	% Probability					
2	1	2.78					
3	2	5.56					
4	3	8.33					
5	4	11.11					
6	5	13.89					
7	6	16.67					
8	5	13.89					
9	4	11.11					
10	3	8.33					
11	2	5.56					
12	1	2.78					

Figure 48: The 36 combinations of two dice in craps.

Three craps – a three will scoop 15:1

Any craps – underneath the single bets you will see 'any craps', so a two, three or 12 will win 8:1.

There are other bets, but this is quite enough to get you understanding and playing. The principle is, if you don't understand a bet then don't risk it.

A few bets not to make

Once you can work your way around the table is seems a lot less complex than at first sight. Some of the bets will look very tempting, especially if you seem to be on a streak of good luck, or if a shooter seems to have good control of the dice. Yet just remember about luck. It is elusive and you are far better to trust to mathematical probability and odds.

Big 6 *and* **Big 8** – I mention these in this section and not in the section above because I would not advise you to play these. These are at the bottom corners, a six or an eight. You win even money if a six or eight is rolled before a seven.

The odds look OK, but you will win less than if you simply placed your bet.

Twelve craps *or* **Boxcars** – that 30:1 is mighty tempting, but consider the odds. You have a 1 in 36 chance of it being made. If you bet $1 on 36 throws you would spend $36. Yet you will only recoup $30. You are onto a loser before you start.

Snake-eyes – the same argument goes for a double one. Don't let the psychology of the table fool you.

Craps manners

From our discussion so far you may be fully put off ever playing the game or fired with enthusiasm to try your hand. You should be aware that as with most things in life there is a code of conduct attached to craps playing.

First and foremost make sure that you understand the rudiments of the game. While people may be willing to give a few words of encouragement be aware that craps is a fast game and you cannot expect to be taught at the table.

Be polite and do not barge into a game. If there is space at the table then you may be allowed to join.

People go to the tables to play, not to chat. It is not the place to engage someone in conversation. Most players will be concentrating and trying to work out their bets.

While you will undoubtedly have seen actors blowing on dice to breathe luck into them, it is not hygienic. The next player may not want to use those dice and will probably ask for new ones. You just don't do it.

Another thing that you should never do is to offer advice about a bet. Players like to do their own thing and follow their instincts. They are unlikely to want to have their instinct questioned or criticised.

Be sporting. This means don't screech or shout out to Lady Luck (if you believe in her despite all that I have said) to make a particular number come up. Other players may think that you have influenced the dice to land that way and cause them to lose money on the bet. You may say that is simply being illogical, yet if it is, then why would you try to influence the dice by calling out.

Chapter 14

A Few More Games Of Risk

The games in this chapter have all been used for gambling over the years. Many still are, but do be careful and have an awareness that the odds on some are quite heavily in favour of the bank or house.

THE BIG SIX OR THE WHEEL OF FORTUNE

This used to be a fairground game that looks fun and looks as if the lucky player could win well. In fact, it really is one to avoid.

It consists of a vertically placed wheel of about 1.5 metres diameter which has 52 or 54 segments divided by spokes. Each segment will have three dice combinations, or colours or various denominations of money. I remember seeing one at a fair when I was a youngster, one segment of which had a pristine twenty pound note that looked to be up for grabs; only it wasn't, of course.

This game is available in casinos in the USA and the UK and it will always attract people.

The segments represent *some* of the possible 216 combinations that you could throw with three dice. Some of the combinations are repeated. You are then invited to bet on a dice number from one to six. If one of the numbers comes up you get paid 1:1, a double gets 2:1 and a triple 3:1.

The seeming profusion of dice on the wheel makes it look a pretty decent bet, yet the organisation of the numbers is such that there are likely to be a mere seven segments where one die will match; four when a double will match and four when a triple will match. That means respectively 7/54 for even money, 4/54 for double and 4/54 for triple money.

Do you see what I mean, that is an awful lot of opportunity to lose. Yet it can be a fun sort of game at charity events, and in that spirit be prepared to give to charity and have some fun. As a gambling venture, avoid it.

P'AT CHA OR GRASPING EIGHT

(8d6)
This is an old Chinese game using a grid with six numbers and eight dice.

How to play P'at Cha

Make a grid with six boxes each containing a number from one to six. One player is the banker and the others place bets on the grid.

A player rolls eight dice. If three of a kind come up the banker pays 8:1. If six of a kind come up the banker pays out 16:1.

All other bets lose.

Just consider that with eight dice there are 1,679,616 possible combinations!

CHO-HAN BAKUCHI

(2d6)

This is a traditional Japanese gambling game. It originated in the Eighteenth Century and was played by crime gangs. It is still a favoured game of the Yakuza in Japan. It is traditionally played on a woven mat with players sitting in a circle. Two dice are used in a bamboo dice bowl or dice cup.

How to play Cho-Han Bakuchi

One player is the dealer. He shakes the dice in the cup and turns it over and leaves it in place. The players then bet on whether the total of the dice will be Cho (even) or Han (odd).

Winners are paid out in proportion to the number who bet correctly. If no one bets correctly, the dealer acts as the bank and keeps the money. If it is an organised game then the house may take an agreed edge.

THREES

(5d6)

This game is also called Bender's Delight, indicating its use as a student drinking game.

The aim is to score the lowest that you can over a number of rounds whereby at least one die is kept aside each time. Paper and pencils may be needed to record each players score.

Threes count as zero.

Five threes wins, but five sixes, called shooting the moon, would also win, but is subservient to 5 threes.

How to play threes

Each player puts an ante in the centre and rolls a high roll for the person to start.

Each player rolls all five dice and keeps back as many as he wants, but at least one each time. A three is zero so is the most desirable. The next player goes, and so on until each player has set aside five dice. Their total low count wins the pot.

Five threes automatically win, if that is rolled at any point, as will shooting the moon, at five sixes.

STRUNG FLOWERS

(3d6)
This is another old Chinese game, called Sz'ng Luk. It is a gambling game with colourful terminology.

How to play Strung Flowers

One player acts as the banker and covers the other players bets. The bets are strung, meaning they are placed in units of three. This is because payments can depend upon differences in the 'points'. To understand this you need to understand the full method of play and scoring.

The banker is decided by high roll. So, once the banker is decided bets are placed. The banker then rolls the three dice.

The banker wins if he rolls:

- three of a kind
- a pair and a six
- a run of four, five, six. This is known as '*strung flowers*'

The banker loses if he rolls:

- any pair and a one. This is known as '*ace negative*'
- a run of one, two, three. This is known as '*dancing the dragon*'

If the banker throws any pair and a number other than a one or a six then the other players take turns to roll.

The players win if they roll:

- any pair and a one
- a run of one, two, three

Now to explain the 'point'. This is any number other than a one or six after a pair has been rolled. Thus it can be a two, three, four or five. A bet that depends on the points will be paid according to how much it varies from the banker's point. By one point wins a third, by two wins a double and by three wins the whole bet.

COIN AND DIE
(1d6)

This is a game to avoid, because it is one that favours the banker. I have seen it played in bars and by groups on a train.

How to play coin and die
Don't play this for money, especially if you are given no chance in being the dealer.

The dealer flips a coin and tosses a die at the same time. If the coin shows a head, then the player wins double the amount shown on the die. If it comes up tails the player loses and the dealer receives four units plus the value on the die.

You might think that sounds good, because if the coin is a head and the die a six, you the player would receive 12 units. On the other hand, if it was tails the dealer would only receive 10 units. Similarly a head and a five would give the player 10, while a tails would only give the dealer a nine. But every other bet would give the dealer an edge.

Altogether the dealer has an edge of almost 3.5 per cent.

SEVENS
(6d6)

As you know seven is the easiest number to roll with two dice. In this game players have to remove any two dice that add up to seven. The aim is to achieve the highest score that one can.

How to play sevens
High roll for the dealer. The dealer then rolls all six dice and removes any two dice that add up to seven. The remaining dice are added up. If the dealer is happy that they have a high enough total, and that they do not add up to seven. If not he may throw the remaining dice, but again, any that add up to seven must be removed. He may throw again or choose to stick. The other players must then try to beat his final total, but are only permitted as many rolls as the dealer had.

OVER AND UNDER SEVENS
(2d6)

In this game two dice are thrown and players bet on whether the score will be seven, or under seven or over seven.

How to play Over and Under Sevens
This can be done with a grid of thee boxes labelled:

[-] [7] [+]

Bets are placed against the bank. Under and over bets both get paid out on even money and seven gets paid out at 4:1.

Now that seems a good sort of bet, because from what you know, a seven is the easiest number to roll. It is because you know that, that you may fall into the trap of thinking it is going to come up a lot of the time. Well, the fact is that it is the easiest to make, but if you refer back to the odds in Figure 20 or 48 you will see that while the probability of making seven is 16.67, that means that the probability of not making it is 83.33.

That means that the natural odds against making it are 5:1.

KLONDIKE
I have always had a soft spot for this game, because the name just conjures up images of Charlie Chaplin in the great silent film *The Gold Rush*. It is a tale about the little tramp going off to the Klondike during the Gold Rush of 1898. There he becomes snowbound in a cabin with a fellow prospector.

There are two variants of Klondike, the simple counter Klondike played with five dice and the quite different casino version played with ten dice.

Counter Klondike
(5d6)

This is a simple one throw game which was played by miners, prospectors and gamblers throughout the Old West and in the mining areas of the Klondike. It is quite similar to poker dice, but is played with ordinary dice.

How to play counter Klondike
High roll to decide the dealer. The aim is to throw a high hand using dice in the order of: one (highest) six, five, four, three, two.

If a die is not used in a combination then it is discounted. If a player matches the dealer, then the dealer wins.

The hands are in order of supremacy:

Five of a kind
Four of a kind
Full house – three of a kind and a pair
Three of a kind
Two pairs
One pair

Betting is usually evens, but if there are many players then shift the dealer and play proportions.

Casino Klondike
(10d6)

This is similar, but with an additional component of beating two aces.

The game is played on a table laid out with win and lose boxes and 'beat two aces' boxes.

Players lay their bets, to win, to lose or to beat two aces. The dealer throws five dice and makes the best hand available from those five dice. The first player then throws and, if betting to win, must beat the hand. If to lose, he must throw less than the dealer's hands. And if playing to beat two aces, he must throw at least two pairs, regardless of the dealer's hand.

You should know that the odds against beating the two aces is 1.25:1.

Chapter 15

Board Games

It is not surprising that archaeologists have been able to give us some insight into the board games that were played in ancient days. By definition a board game was played on a board and would therefore have been regarded as a possession of great value. The wealthy and leisured classes in antiquity would, therefore, take such things into their tombs in order to be able to play again in the afterlife. We have therefore been able to chart the history of many games, or at least have a good stab at reconstructing the rules and method by which they were played. Of the more ancient games which were simply played with dice we are less sure, although it is a fair guess that many of the games outlined in this book have found their way down through the ages by simple oral tradition and re-enactment each time they have been played.

Games psychology

As we have already seen in this book people have been playing games for as long as recorded history. Indeed, from archaeological finds of knucklebones used in the dim distant past, games were played long before the invention of writing.

In the last few chapters we have also looked at several types of both board and non-board dice games. From now on we are going to deal exclusively with board games. It would seem entirely appropriate therefore to take a little look at games psychology.

Games are generally about competition. Although many people profess to have no competitive spirit whatsoever, is that really the case? Do they simply play a game out of sociability or do they secretly strive to win? And if they do win do they inwardly smile?

Most people play a game and attempt to win. It is a natural thing to try to show one's adeptness, one's skill and one's intelligence. Even in a game of chance in which dice are used they will try hard to pass the finishing line first or to reach the home square before their opponents.

The fact is that a game is a substitute for activity. It is a way of reducing some aspect of real life to a board, a grid or an imaginary field. The roll of the dice adds that unpredictability that is such a feature of life itself.

There are broadly two types of board game that I want to discuss. One is a chasing game and the other is a strategy game. While there may be some overlap, yet there are sufficient differences to differentiate them.

Firstly, chase games. Essentially the aim is for a player to navigate his way over a board, each move being determined by the roll of one or more dice, overcoming or evading obstacles along the way in order to get one or all of his markers or board pieces across the finishing line. These can usually be played by two or more people.

Then there are strategic or tactical games. The aim here is to mobilise one's pieces, again being determined on the roll of dice, in order to overcome one's opposition or remove him or her from the board. These can sometimes be played by more than two people, but more often they are games to be played by two people.

When we watch a game we become engrossed in it because we utilise unconscious mental mechanisms. With a lot of physical sports that we watch in an arena or on a sports field, we operate the mental mechanism of *sublimation*. This means that we transform a socially unacceptable behaviour into a lesser one that is acceptable. You may not think it, but most sports have a combative edge to them, rather like the gladiatorial combats of Roman days. Human beings are basically quite aggressive creatures, yet as we have developed into societies we have moved away from outright aggression and substituted sport. Instead of fighting we channel our aggressive drive into a game or sport.

The second mental mechanism is *identification*. When you spectate at a sport you identify with one team or the other. Once again, it is analogous to the crowd at the Roman spectaculars in the Coliseum, you choose a champion and you back them.

Board games are not as different as you might imagine. You select a piece or a player and you identify with that character. You sublimate a chase in real life, or a battle with the team or pieces on the board game. You want them to win and you want your opponent's pieces to fail.

As we shall see in a later chapter, other board games have developed in the last few decades to permit another human characteristic to enter into a board game. That is creativity. In modern role-playing and war-gaming, players actually construct the game or the world they are playing in as they go along.

Dice or no dice

Many board games are played without dice. Games like chess and Go are played in strict move after move, each player's next move being a logical reaction to the opponent's last move.

The element of chance, of course, is introduced by the use of a die or of two or more dice. Here the number of games is countless.

Some games combine strategy with luck. Why is that? Is the strictly player against player type of game harder? Does the use of the dice even the odds and give the less able player a better chance? Or is it just that people like the uncertainty?

Go

The Chinese game of Weiqi, or Wei-Hai, which means 'encirclement', is commonly called Go. It is a game that has been played for at least two thousand years in China in a form that has not changed. No dice are required.

It is played on a 19x19 grid with black and white stones. Players start with a clean board and alternately place stones on the intersections of the grid, the aim being to gain as much of the grid as one can, by encircling the opponent's individual stones so that they are overpowered and subdued.

It is an incredibly skilful game and is played by around 30 million people around the world.

Chaturanga

This is another ancient game that was played in India in about the Sixth Century. It was played on a board called 'Ashtapada', which consisted on an 8x8 grid, some of the squares having special markings, although their significance is not known today. It was played by two players and was played without dice. It is thought to be the root of games like chess and the Japanese game Shogi.

Each player had several pieces which are similar to those used in chess today. They comprised the king, the counsellor (which seems to have become the queen in chess), the chariot (which equates with the rook), the elephant (the bishop), the horse (the knight), and a row of foot-soldiers (pawns in modern day chess).

A slightly later version of this game called 'Chaturaji', meaning four kings, was played in the Eleventh Century. In this version four people played on the same board, using dice to determine moves.

Chess

The great game of chess surely needs no introduction. It is derived from Chaturanga and is a great game of strategies played by two people on an 8x8 board with 16 pieces each. It may, therefore, have been around since about the Seventh Century AD. The game found its way to the Arab world where it became known as Shatranj and was played for several centuries in an unchanged manner. It had thus changed from being a chase and tactical game, to a straight combat, as if by two armies.

By about 1000 AD it had spread to Europe and quickly became a game favoured by the nobility. At that time the pawns could only be moved one square at a time and the queen could only move diagonally one square at a time. As you can imagine, that would make it a very different game. In around 1475 a major change took part when the game was changed in Spain. The queen was given greater powers and soon became the most powerful piece on the board.

Since this is a book about dice we shall in fact return to this in the chapter when we consider Dice Chess.

The Lewis Chess set

In 1831 after an exceptionally high tide at Uig on the Island of Lewis in the Outer Hebrides a crofter was chasing a cow over the beach. A sandbank had collapsed and a stone cairn was revealed to him. Inside it he found 78 chess pieces carved from Walrus tusks. He sold them to the British Museum for what seemed to him a princely sum of £80.

These were identified as being chess pieces from eight sets, of Norse origin, but depicting both church dignitaries and Norse warriors.

The famous Isle of Lewis Chess set is now housed in the national Museum of Scotland in Edinburgh.

Pachisi
(5d2)

This is another game that originated in ancient India, possibly more than two millennia ago, although its actual date cannot be stated with certainty. It is a chase or race game played out on a cross shaped grid. It has been described as the national board game of India!

It is said that the Mogul emperor Akbar (1542–1606), the third emperor of the Mogul dynasty used to play pachisi on a grand life-size scale with beautiful women selected from his harem as pachisi pieces. He had giant pachisi courts on stages set up in his palaces at Agra and Allahabad.

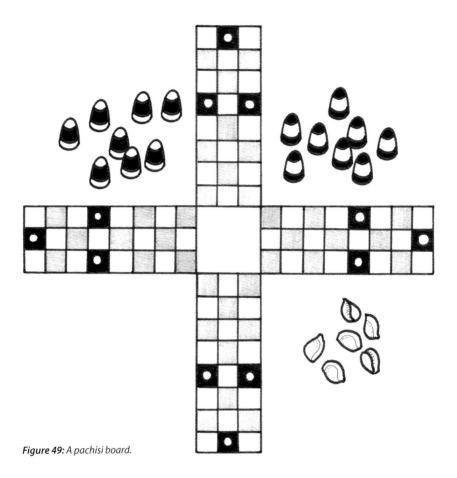

Figure 49: A pachisi board.

The simple and less elaborate pachisi means of play was on a 'board' traditionally made of squares of embroidered cloth sewn together so that there was a central large home square called *the 'charkoni'* with four arms of a cross extending, each from one of the square's sides, so that each arm had three rows of eight squares. Four people, usually in two teams of two players would play. One team would play with yellow and black pieces and the others with red and green pieces.

The name pachisi means 25, which relates to the largest score that could be obtained. Either long wooden dice were used, or traditionally five cowrie shells. Cowrie shells are relatively flat shells; one side (the back) being smooth and the underside having teeth.

Each player would start with four pieces or counters, which would be placed in the home square. The aim would be to get all of the counters round the whole grid, starting up the middle column of their arm and then going anti-clockwise down the outside, then all the way round the cross before arriving back at the top of the arm. Then they go again down the middle arm to the home square.

There are three safe or castle squares on each arm, which if a piece occupies them is safe from capture.

Pieces are moved according to the throw of the cowrie shells so that the number is determined by the number of toothed sides that show uppermost once they have been cast.

0 showing = 25
1 showing = 1
2 showing = 2
3 showing = 3
4 showing = 4
5 showing = 5

Both a five and a 25 permit an extra piece to enter or you can move another piece one extra position. Also, you get to go again.

Sometimes six cowrie shells would be used and indeed, if so then you could play with a single die, making the six equal in value to 25 points.

If a player lands on a castle square then that is his while he is there and another player of the opposite team may not land there. If a player lands on another square already occupied by his opponent then his piece is captured and he has to return to charkoni. He then has to start again, but the person who captured him gets to play again.

To reach charkoni each time you have to do so by throwing the exact number.

Ludo
(1d6)

This is a game that was derived from Pachisi during the days of the British Raj. A variant was patented in 1896. It is simpler than pachisi and has become a family favourite for succeeding generations.

The grid is another cross with a central home square and four arms containing three columns of six squares. The central rows of each terminate in an arrowhead in the home square to designate the direction they must go to reach home. There are also four large areas where the pieces have to start from. While they are there they are not yet on the board. The actual starting square is the first of the coloured squares on their arm. Each player has four counters of an appropriate colour.

Figure 50: *Ludo.*

Up to four players can use the board at any time. Play starts with a high roll (high roll on the die goes first). Each player must then throw a six to get a piece on the board, meaning onto the starting square. From then on they move each piece clockwise around the perimeter of the board and then down the middle column to the home square. At the end they must make it home in the exact number.

Throwing a one or a six any time after starting entitles a player to move a piece onto their starting square, provided it is not occupied. Each six will get the player another move, but if he throws three sixes in a row he misses a turn.

If one lands on a square occupied by your opponent then you capture his piece and it has to go back to the starting area to begin again. On the other hand you may not land on a square occupied by one of your own counters.

The winner is the person who is first to get all four of his pieces home.

Snakes and Ladders
(1d6)

Most people will have played Snakes and Ladders, yet most will probably not have realised that it is a morality game. Like Ludo it comes from the days of the British Raj and is derived from an old Indian game called 'Moksha-patamu', which dates back to the Second Century BC. It was used by religious leaders to teach their children the difference between good and evil, and to appreciate the dangers of the various sins, like greed and pride, as opposed to the virtues such as honesty.

The ladders lead upwards to heaven and the snakes show the descent into the nether regions.

The game is played on a grid consisting of 100 squares, numbered from one to 100; one being the starting square and 100 being the end. Different length ladders take you up to higher levels and different sized snakes take you down similarly great or small distances. You only go up a ladder and down a snake.

Up to six players can use the board at a time and each player has a single counter. A high roll starts the game. A six gets a player another turn. If a player lands on a square where another player has already landed, then you miss your next turn.

Crown and Anchor
(3d6 – special faced Crown and Anchor dice)

This is a game that has been a favourite of seamen. It is said to have originated in Bermuda, invented by British Navy sailors during the Eighteenth Century. It is a gambling game. This is quite a simple game, but be aware of odds! It is a game in favour of the banker.

The grid is a large canvas or felt sheet divided into six squares, each bearing the symbol of one of the four card suits, clubs, hearts, diamonds and spades and a crown and an anchor.

Three dice are used similarly bearing the four card suits and a crown and an anchor. They are usually kept in a shaker-cage, which is a basket or metal cage shaped like an hourglass, so there is no handling of them.

One player is designated as the banker on the first game by rolling a die. The first to get a crown is the banker and the other or others are players. The person to his left is banker next time, if it is agreed to rotate.

Players make a bet by placing a coin or token or whatever is being used, on one of the squares. The banker has to cover and accept all bets. The shaker-cage is then shaken or turned so that the dice are rolled. If any dice come up

Figure 51: Crown and Anchor.

with the appropriately bet upon signs, then the banker pays out. He pays out even money for one die, 2:1 for two dice and 3:1 for three dice. If none show up he keeps all bets.

If the banker does not change to another person then the players had better be prepared to lose.

If you place any one single bet:

Matches	Possible combinations
0	125
1	75
2	15
3	1
Total	216

A little simple arithmetic tells you that any double will occur 90 times out of 216 rolls and a triple a mere six times. No brilliant odds for the player, but good for the bank.

Chuck-a-luck and Grand Hazard
(3d6)

This game is almost the same as Crowns and Anchors, in that it also is played with a shaker-cage. It is more out of historical interest nowadays, since it is rarely played. It also used to be called 'birdcage' for obvious reasons. It was reckoned to be uncheatable, which is why Professor JB Rhine used it in his famous ESP experiments, which I touched on in Chapter 10.

It was also a favoured game in the days of the Old West, when it was played with three simple dice and a simple arrangement of six numbers on a felt sheet. The game was notorious for helping the unwary to lose money and so it was named Chuck-a-luck, or chucker luck.

Interestingly, before the shaker-cage or birdcage was introduced, Chuck-a-luck was played in the old saloons using a 'hazard horn'. This was a *tinhorn* that was generally used to play Grand Hazard, another gambling that was played in slightly more up-market gambling houses. It was actually nothing like the English game of Hazard that would eventually evolve into the great American favourite of craps. It was in fact pretty similar to Chuck-a-luck in that it also used three dice and six numbers on a sheet or board with various odds added at various points to make it look both complex and enticing. Again, the house would pay out evens for one number, 2:1 for a double and 3:1 for a triple.

The tinhorn was a metal cone-shaped horn through which the dice were dropped. Inside it had projections which ensured that the dice fell out at random. The first ones were made of leather, but these were replaced, especially by small gambling houses or by independents with metal tinhorns. In time the term came to be used for any individual who believed they had superior knowledge or aptitude than they actually possessed. Hence the phrase so often used in the West – 'tinhorn gambler'.

Rancho Notorious

One of the great western movies of 1952 was *Rancho Notorious*, starring Marlene Dietrich, who plays Altar Keane the femme fatale owner of Chuck-a-luck, the outlaw ranch on the Mexican border.

It was originally to have been called The Legend of Chuck-a-luck, but Howard Hughes, the owner of the studio changed the name. It was probably a good decision, for the name may have given too much of the story away.

Modern board games

There are many popular board games nowadays which employ dice. The use of the dice is merely a means of introducing obstacles and potential penalties to the player in order to hamper progress through skill. The following have all achieved cult followings over the years.

Monopoly – which is a game designed to show one's entrepreneurial skills as you seek to take over fiscal control of a city

Cluedo – which is a game designed to show off one's deductive skills by unmasking a murderer

Trivial Pursuits – in which a person or team aim to show intellectual dominance by answering questions across a spread of subjects

Risk – in which one player strives for world domination

Chapter 16

Dice Chess

(1 or 2 d6)

The game of chess is a paradox. It is simple to learn; you can learn the rudiments well enough to play the game in less than an hour. On the other hand it can take a lifetime to play well. Most people will learn to play up to a certain level and progress no further. A few seem blessed with ability from an early age and may well achieve grandmaster status at a relatively young age.

Figure 52: Dice Chess.

It is game that people associate with great intelligence and assume that in order to play it you have to have a special sort of brain, an aptitude in mathematics or science. In fact, that is not necessarily the case. A good chess player may be simply that, someone who can see the game and be able to think several moves ahead, taking lots of possible counter moves into account.

Of course, much will depend upon the speed at which the game is played, for when time is limited one actually has to think not only at a different pace, but in a different way.

This book is of course about dice, so I do not intend talking for long about chess other than to describe some of the rudiments of it which I am sure will help if you decide to play the fascinating game of dice chess.

But first let me talk about that fascinating business of the way you think when playing games. It is quiet relevant to chess.

Heuristics and algorithms

This might sound as if it is going to get complicated, but fear not. It may actually help you to appreciate both the game of chess and that of the variant that I want to discuss in this chapter, dice chess.

If you had unlimited time to play a game of chess, or at least a lengthy time to ponder, such as people used to do when they played chess by mail in the old days, you ought to be able to plan your moves. You would consider all possibilities and work out the best possible next move. It would be a logical choice. These sorts of games used to go on for months.

The sort of thought process involved in making those moves is called algorithmic. An algorithm is a linear sequence of thoughts that will arrive at a logical and accurate conclusion. The algorithm was named after the Persian mathematician, Al-Khawarizmi (790–840 AD), who invented algebra. This sort of thought is cold logic when there is a lot of time and the problem is clear and well defined. Most computer programs are algorithm based.

If however, you do not have a lot of time to make a decision and the problem is not clearly defined, then you tend to think heuristically. This means that you find the best answer possible in the available time and you operate a sort of unconscious rule of thumb type of thought.

Heuristic thinking is a sort of quick short-cut thinking that people use once they have reached a certain level of skill in an endeavour. The more skilled you become the less you need to go through the complex process of thought. It is almost as if you suddenly see the answer. It is typical of the sort of sixth sense that people develop in their chosen careers. The longer you do something, the more experienced you are, then the more reliable will be your heuristic thinking.

One problem about heuristic thinking, of course, is that while it is often very accurate, it can also be at times wide of the mark. This is because heuristics tend to be unconsciously biased. We are biased in our thinking, so when you go on hunches, they tend to express your own bias.

Experience teaches how to solve things quickly
The mathematician George Polya taught that experience teaches people how to solve problems. This worked especially when there was no obvious algorithm. The repetition of solving problems induced a heuristic or an unconscious rule of thumb. Thus when faced with problems an individual would be able to quickly recognise possible solutions. He wrote a ground-breaking book *How to Solve* which was published in 1957, and it is still in print today.

Heuristics and algorithms in games

Taking a long time over a game, any game, makes it fairly boring for spectators. It also makes the game lose some of its magic for the players. In order to keep it competitive a game needs to be played fairly crisply and evenly. With chess that means limiting the amount of time between moves.

This will automatically limit the amount of algorithmic thinking. Some people are quick thinkers, of course, and may be able to rattle through their algorithms, while others may get flustered. Getting flustered is never a help in any game, so instead of letting time upset your stride you sometimes need to go with instincts and gut feelings. The person who does this is often going to win because they will develop good instincts. They can be very difficult to beat.

Playing dice chess may help you to think heuristically and improve your general chess. I will explain how in a few moments.

Deep Blue

In 1997 the computer company IBM developed a chess playing computer called Deep Blue. In a six-game competition it defeated Garry Kasparov the world chess champion. It was a surprising victory, considering that Kasparov had defeated the computer in a six-game competition the previous year. He was denied a rematch, however, as IBM dismantled the computer.

Now, we have talked about odds quite a bit in this book. Although you don't think about odds in terms of chess, they are relevant. It is estimated that from any average position on a chess board there are 38 possible moves. To analyse the implications of six moves by each player would swell the number of possible moves to huge numbers. Numbers so large that you could almost blow a fuse trying to calculate how many, let alone retain them all. And yet, deciding which are good moves and which are bad is the great skill. A computer will not have skill, what it will have is algorithmic capability. Yet even a computer will take time to go through all of the possible moves and discard all the bad moves. In order to discard bad moves it will use a set of algorithms, which means it will go through a set program and those moves that are good will have set criteria that have to be reached, otherwise they are rejected.

This is where heuristics come in to the benefit of the human mind. We tend to operate heuristically when time is short. And in analysing all the options in a game, time is always short, since there is not always a right answer, but a range of possibilities. Heuristics are effectively recognition patterns that are arrived at swiftly without going through all of the odds. They are a bit like making guesstimates, which is why they can be, as I mentioned earlier, either extremely accurate or at times wide of the mark.

A world chess champion will beat a chess playing computer unless the programmers give the computer the ability to 'think' in the same ways as a human. The nearest they can get is to program in some heuristics or automatic short-cuts.

Heuristics are for fast thinking

If you play chess quickly against a chess computer you have the best chance of winning. You can't compete algorithmically, but heuristically you can. Try it yourself and use the short-cut process to make the computer move almost immediately. It will then give the best available move it has been able to work out. And that is just what you want to do if you have limited time, give the best available move.

You may have seen grandmasters play 20 games of chess all at once, moving from game to game and playing instantly, while the opponent in each match is left to sit and ponder. In fact, if the players just went head to head as quickly as possible, the ordinary player may do better than he expected. This is because he would be thinking heuristically.

The brain shows it

Recent research from Japan confirms that experience changes the way the brain works. A team involved in cognitive brain mapping studied a group of professional Shogi players and compared them with those of another group of amateurs, as they all played Shogi. This is the Japanese form of chess. Both groups were shown various board patterns and asked to make a sequence of rapid moves.

They found that there were two marked differences in the way that the brains of the two groups functioned. Firstly, the professionals instantly activated parts of their brains called the *precuneus* in the parietal lobes, under your crown. Secondly, when forced to make quick moves the experts activated a structure called the *caudate nucleus* in their basal ganglia.

These brain findings correspond with what we think of as intuition, or just good old fashioned 'know-how'. You have to train the brain to become expert in your field, but once you have know-how, your brain just does it without thinking.

This is heuristic learning.

Dice chess

It is not easy handicapping players in chess, as you can in some sports like golf. You can give someone knight's advantage or queen's advantage and play without your knights or your queen. That is a considerable advantage and it will not give much satisfaction to either player.

How to weigh the value of each chess piece
It is an imprecise method, but if you give each piece a point score, then a pawn is about one; a knight or a bishop is about three; a rook is about five and a queen is about nine.

As I mentioned above, you can do it by playing speed chess, but a really fun way is to play dice chess. This will make you think heuristically, because by introducing a dice into the game you allow chance to intervene and it will even the odds between a good player and a lesser able player. Both will have to make moves, but they will be able to make less moves than in standard chess. It will also help your game, because it makes you see and recognise chess patterns.

I will assume that you know how to play the game of chess. I will also assume that you understand chess standard notation as it is now used. I grew up using the old English notation, which is little used these days. Nowadays the international standard notation is the algebraic system. This means that

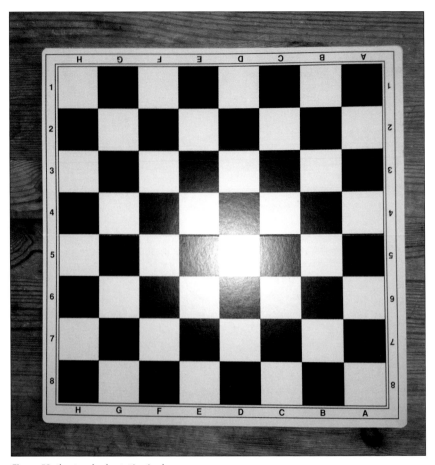

Figure 53: the standard notation in chess.

the squares are labelled **a** to **h** from left to right and then from **1** to **8** from bottom to top. So every square can be identified.

The pieces are also identified by their initial letters, except the knight. Thus, K (king); Q (queen); R (rook); B (bishop); and N (knight, for obvious reasons).

Dice chess is played exactly the same way as standard chess except that before each move a player rolls a die, which will indicate which type of piece he will have to move.

The numbers on the dice represent a piece, as follows:

One   =   pawn
Two   =   knight
Three =   bishop
Four =   rook
Five =   queen
Six   =   king

You can play with either one die or two. If you play with two you have a choice of moves, but one is more restrictive and will result in quicker games. An additional advantage of two dice is that if you roll a double you may play any legal move and can ignore the dice values.

Castling is permitted if you roll a four and a six or any double. It has to be a possible castle move, of course.

To play you roll a die and the highest chooses which colour to play. He rolls first and has to roll either a one or a two, since the game can only start with a pawn or a knight. If he fails to throw either then he misses a move and it is the other person's turn.

The player has to move the piece that is indicated, as long as it is able to move. If it is a King then that has to be moved if it is possible for it to move, otherwise a turn is missed and the other player has a roll of the dice. A King may even have to move to a square that will give checkmate to do so if that is his only move.

You will see that the game is quickfire. You are not permitted a lengthy time to move, since the aim is to be swift. Most games will in fact only last a few minutes and they are good fun.

The three parts of the game

If you have not played much chess you may not be aware that chess generally falls into three parts. This is just as true in dice chess and if you have some idea about what sort of tactics to adopt then it will help you in your standard game.

I mention this because a lot of people do not like to expose themselves to the rigour of the chess board. Many people are put off because they think they could be humiliated or crushed. Yet with dice chess the advantage of the good player will be trimmed back. That is why you should try and adopt a few basic tactics.

The opening game

Whole libraries have been written about the different ways to open a game, yet most people restrict themselves to one or two. If you play only a few people they will soon get to know your method. Be aware that there is no such thing as a perfect opening. What you have to try to do is mislead your opponent.

Basically there are two type of opening game – open or closed. Open games aim to quickly develop the game. Closed games want to keep it tight.

When a pawn starts the e4 move, it will tend towards an open game, whereas d4 will be more closed. When you are starting at chess, standard or dice chess, then you are probably as well beginning with e4. Open it up, especially in dice chess.

You may tend to go for a sideways attack in standard chess, yet this is going to be limiting in dice chess.

The middle game

The key here is really to try and get as much action as you can going on in the middle of the board. From there you will have greatest range to hit out at the flanks or advance forward: if you can get your knights and queen into that area of the board. If you get stuck at the sides you may end up with little room to manoeuvre in dice chess.

The endgame

This will come quickly in dice chess. You will probably not get to the cat and mouse stage that can occur in standard chess when you are down to your kings and one or two other pieces. Chance will play a part but if you have managed to open the game, advance centrally and get pieces into the mid-board you have a good chance of victory.

In conclusion

Do not despise dice chess. It will enable you to have a matched game with anyone and it will teach you quick pattern recognition, which will develop heuristic thinking. I would recommend playing a few games with one die to get used to the idea, then play properly with two dice. You will find that it is quick and quite compulsive. Play the best out of three or best out of five.

This is liable to improve your game when you play standard chess. After you have developed a knack try playing a few games of speed chess and I think you will be surprised at how it changes your game.

Good luck.

Chapter 17

Family Dice Games

There are lots of easy dice games that you can play as a family. Most are quite simple and can be played by children of as young as four years of age.

BEETLE
(1d6)

Children love games in which they make or draw things. This is one that young children love and which may stretch their artistic ability.

Any number can play.

You draw a beetle for them to see and draw a ring around each of the body parts. You allot each part a number value, thus:

One   = body
Two   = head
Three = one antenna
Four = one leg
Five = one eye
Six   = tail

To play Beetle
You all start with a pencil and a piece of paper. One die is needed.

Start with a High roll (high die starts). Take turns in the usual way, starting with the person who wins the High roll, then go clockwise. The idea is to build a beetle's body, getting a part for each throw of the die. You have to start with a body, so if you keep rolling a number other than one you can't start. With each part that you gain you draw it on your beetle until the winner cries BEETLE!

HELP YOUR NEIGHBOUR
(2d6 and a pack of playing cards)

This is a neat card and dice game for four players. There is not a high skill level so young children can play. They do find this one great fun.

Four players.

Divide the pack into the four suits and give each player a suit. Throw away the aces and the kings. Thus you will be left with cards running from two to 12 (Jack = 11, Queen = 12).

To play Help your Neighbour

As usual decide on the order by doing a High roll. Each player lays all of their cards in a row, face up in order from two up to queen. Then each player in turn rolls two dice and adds the totals to give a number. They then turn over the card so that it is face down.

If you cannot turn a card over, because you have already done so, then you can help your neighbour on the left, by turning over theirs if it is still face up. This allows the player to keep going, which he does until he either cannot turn over one of his own or one of his neighbour's. He may decide not to help his neighbour, in which case his turn is over and it is up the neighbour to keep going by turning over his cards or his neighbour on his left.

The winner is the person who turns all of his cards over.

BALLOONS
(1d6)

This is another one for young children that can help them recognise numbers and is also good for helping with colours.

Any number can play

Start by drawing six rows of three balloons on several pieces of paper, depending on how many children are playing. Number each balloon, so that your first row is made up of three ones, the second of three twos all the way to six. Also select a different colour for each number

One	=	red
Two	=	orange
Three	=	yellow
Four	=	green
Five	=	blue
Six	=	purple

How to play Balloons
Do a High roll as usual to decide order of play. Each player takes turns to roll the die. For each number they get to colour in an appropriate balloon. The aim is to get all the rows. You can of course vary it depending upon the children's attention spans. You may for example simply decide that the first player to colour in a row wins.

STUCK IN THE MUD
(5D6)

This is a good game for helping young children to add up.
Any number can play.
Each person needs a paper and pencil to do sums.

How to play Stuck in the Mud
A High roll is done as usual. The first player then rolls all five dice. Any twos or fives are stuck in the mud and don't count. They are placed aside and the rest of the dice are thrown again. If there are any twos or fives in this throw then none of the dice count and it is the next person's throw. If no twos or fives are thrown on the first throw then all dice count and are added up. This is added to the player's ongoing total. Similarly, if no twos or fives are thrown on the second throw then the counting dice are added up to go on the on-going score.

 Simply decide how many rounds you will have and at the end the winner is the person with the highest (correct) score.

RUNNING
(6d6)

This is another number recognition game and a good one for helping children with their five times table.
Any number can play.
Each player needs a paper and pencil.

How to play Running
A High roll starts and determines order as usual. The aim is to spot runs of numbers. Each die that forms part of a run scores five points, so that a run of three – two, three, four would score 15.

 Decide upon a winning target, usually of 100.

PIG
(1 or 2d6)

This is an old chestnut of a game. It is really simple in that players don't score when they roll a one. It does teach the rudiments of tactics.

Any number can play

How to play Pig
Either one or two dice can be used. Young children will cope with one die, but two is more fun and you may find that your children literally squeal with excitement the faster you play it.

A High roll starts as usual. The first player then rolls the die or the dice. If a one is rolled then the hand is over for that player and they make no score. Anything else scores and they may go on scoring until a one is rolled, in which case they lose their entire score for the hand, or they choose to stick. In that case that score goes towards their ongoing total.

Children may show their basic personality in this game, in that the risk takers will soon become apparent.

BOTTOMS UP
(3d6)

This is a good one for showing children the principle of the opposite faces totalling seven.

Any number can play

How to Play Bottoms Up
After a High roll to determine who starts, each player takes it in turn to throw the three dice. They then have to add the total up and are given the chance of moving one die so that the bottom is facing up. They are not allowed to turn it over to look first, so they have to work out what will be on the bottom of each die.

That figure gives their total for that hand. It is then the next person's go. They continue until a target, 100 perhaps, is reached.

PLUS AND MINUS
(5d6)

Here is another great dice game that helps children learn how to add and subtract.

Any number can play.

The aim is to get the highest total you can on each round to get the highest score that you can, each player using the same routine of arithmetic.

How to play Plus and Minus

A High roll is done as usual to determine who goes first. Generally select a number of rounds you want to play.

Each player rolls the dice four times, like this:

- First roll all five dice, then select two of them in order to add them together to give a starting number. (Plus)
- Put the first two dice aside and roll the remaining three. Select one and subtract it from the total. (Minus)
- Put that dice with the first two and roll the two remaining dice. Select one die and add it to the total. (Plus)
- Put that die aside and roll the last die, subtracting it from the total. (Minus)

This is the first score. Now it is the next person's turn. The winner is the person with the highest total after the five rounds, or however many were chosen.

MOUNTAINEER
(3d6)

This is a good one to help children become familiar with numbers and helps with simple arithmetic.

Each person starts with a sheet of paper on which they 'draw' a mountain by starting at the base on the left and writing increasing numbers from one to 12, and continuing down the other side to one.

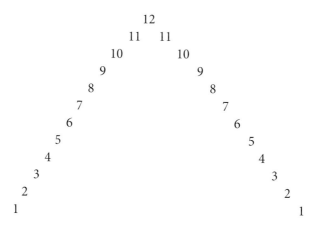

How to play Mountaineer

High roll as usual to start the game off. Each player takes turns to roll three dice. They have to climb the mountain, in the set order. So they have to start with a one, then a two and so on. The way that they make each number can be with a single die, an addition of two or even all three. They can also use one die more than once if they can accommodate it.

For example, if one has already climbed up to number three, then on the next turn they roll a two, four, and five, then they can move up four, five, six and seven, because four and five are numbers shown. Then four plus two is six, and two plus five is seven.

The winner is the first person to ascend and descend the mountain using all numbers.

YACHT
(5d6)

This is a scoring game that is a lot of fun for the whole family. It can be played by any number of people.

There is a commercial game called Yahtze, which is similar with pre-printed cards.

Each person needs a score sheet recording how well they score on the following:

- Yacht (five of a kind)   [max score 50]
- Long straight   five numbers in sequence (1,2,3,4,5 or 2,3,4,5,6) [score 30]
- Short straight   four numbers in sequence (1,2,3,4 or 2,3,4,5 or 3,4,5,6) [score 20]
- Four of a kind   [max score 24]
- Full house   three of a kind and a pair [max score 28]
- Choice   any five dice [score whatever value]
- Sixes   [max score 30]
- Fives   [max score 25]
- Fours   [max score 20]
- Threes   [max score 15]
- Twos   [max score 10]
- Ones   [max score 5]

How to play Yacht

Each player takes it in turn to roll five dice. In each round they can throw three times to improve their score. The aim is to fill in a row on each of the scores. Once they have filled in a row it cannot be changed in any way or moved. It is, therefore a tactical game.

At the end of the 12 rounds the scores are added up and the winner is the person with the highest score.

MAH JONG
(3d6)

According to some sources Mah Jong has been played by the Chinese since the days of Confucius. In fact, it is a relatively new game dating back just a hundred years or so, although it may well have been based on a far older game. It has, however been extremely popular and there are Chinese, Japanese and British rules. It is a mix of luck and skill.

It is usually played by four people, who play 16 hands. They actually play four rounds, each one representing a wind or a direction. East begins, followed by South, then West and finally North.

They start with the roll of Mah Jong dice.

One hundred and forty four pictured tiles are stacked to represent a wall. This is formed from 18 stacks, which are then broken so that each player receives 13 tiles, the remainder staying in the centre of the playing area.

Players take turns to play draw and discard tiles, which are like dominoes with wonderful pictures on them, until one player wins with a hand of four combinations of three tiles and a pair of matching tiles.

Chapter 18

Backgammon

(2d6 plus one large 'doubling cube')

As we saw at the start of this book backgammon is one of the very earliest board games that we have evidence for. It seems probably that it dates back to around three millennia BC, which would make it an astonishing 5,000 years old. Truly, that would be a testament to the ingenuity of the first game inventors.

It is a chase and tactics game.

The Backgammon board

Backgammon is a game for two players. A board is used consisting of 24 triangular shapes of alternating colour (usually just black and white), which are referred to as points.

The board has two sides, which are divided by the fold in the board or the hinge section, which is called the bar. It is actually an integral part of the game as we shall see when we come to describe the way the game is played.

There are four quadrants on the board, referred to as the home board and the outer board for each player.

Each of the points is numbered from one to 12 (although most boards do not actually have these printed on them, but the numbering is standard). The first point is in the player's own home board and the final point is in the opponent's home board. The player's 24 point is the opponent's one point, and the player's one point is the opponent's 24 point.

The set up

Each player has 15 pieces according to which colour he is playing. The initial set up is as follows:

- Two pieces on each 24 point
- Five pieces on each 13 point
- Three pieces on each 8 point
- Five pieces on each 6 point

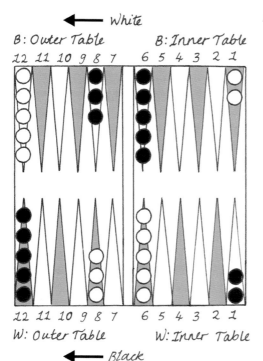

Figure 54: backgammon board.

Each player requires two standard dice and a dice pot.

A large doubling cube is also required with the numbers 2, 4, 8, 16, 32 and 64 on its faces rather than standard dice numbering. Its purpose is to double stakes at appropriate times, as we shall see.

The aim of the game

Quite simply the object is to move all of your pieces round the board into your own home board and then to 'bear them off'. A player can only start to bear off once he has moved all of his pieces into his home board. The first person to bear off all of his pieces wins the game.

Moves depend upon the roll of the dice, so knowledge of the odds on throwing combinations of two dice is definitely advantageous!

Both players will be aiming to do the same and they will tactically try to block and impede their opponent and send various pieces back to the bar if they can.

At the start of the game stakes are placed per point and at various times it is possible to use the doubling cube to double the stakes. This is very relevant at the end of the game.

Rather like chess the game of backgammon does not take long to learn, but it takes a long time to master. Various styles of play and various tactics can be used.

The basics of backgammon

First of all understand the direction of play. Essentially, white moves clockwise and black moves anti-clockwise. They both move from higher numbers to lower numbers.

As you look at Figure 54 it will become clear. As the board is set up with white at the bottom and black at the top, white will move from black's inner table left across black's outer table, then down to white's outer table and then into the inner table. Black will do the reverse and begin in white's home table, then move to *his right* into the outer table then up and round into black's outer table before reaching his own inner table.

Each player has two dice and they should use a dice pot to prevent dice control. Once the game is started they move according to the value of the dice. A player can use each die to move one piece that value of points or he can use the total value of both dice to move a piece as far as possible. Alternately, he can use the value on the second die to move another piece that number of points.

Whenever a player throws a double, that is called a '*doublet*', and it means that both dice have their values doubled. He can either choose to move a single piece double the number of either dice, or he can add them together and double the value. Or he can in fact move four pieces, since he theoretically has four numbers instead of two to play with.

He must attempt to use all numbers if he can, which may not be possible if he has been successfully blocked. But he must try and use the highest numbers. If he cannot move, then play passes to his opponent.

A point is said to be open when it is not occupied by two or more of his opponent's pieces. If a player has occupied a point with two or more pieces then that point is '*made*'. The other player may not land on it.

If a point has a single piece on it, then it is called a '*blot*'. If it is landed on by the opponent, then it is said to be '*hit*', and the player that was originally there is taken off and placed on '*the bar*'.

Once a piece is on the bar then it will have to be re-entered into the game on the player's turn by starting at the appropriate number from the opponent's home board. If it cannot be entered then he misses a go. He must not attempt to move any other piece until all of his pieces are on the board.

A point is '*blocked*' when a player has two or more pieces on it. Only he can land on it. His opponent may move past it, but cannot land on it.

'*Bearing off*' begins once all pieces are in the home board. The aim is to get all 15 pieces off first. If he throws higher numbers than the points he has his pieces on, then he moves them from the next highest point.

The game is won when all 15 of one player's pieces have been borne off. If the other player managed to get at least one of his pieces off then it is called a '*single game*'. He pays one stake, or if the doubling cube was used, then the value that had been agreed and is showing.

If the other player had not managed to bear off any pieces then the game is called a '*gammon*'. The winner receives double, meaning two stakes, or double the doubling cube vales.

If the other player has a piece left in the winner's inner table or still on the bar, then it is '*backgammon*' and he pays triple.

Doubling

As mentioned earlier, a stake is agreed at the start of the game. Say it is a dollar. If both players roll the same number at the start of the game with a single die, which is how the game begins, then the stake is automatically doubled.

The doubling cube was introduced to the game in the 1920s to add a little spice. When a player thinks he has the upper hand, then at the start of his turn before he rolls the dice he can offer to double the stake. The opponent can refuse, in which case he forfeits the game and pays the stake. If he accepts, then the doubling cube is turned to show a two.

The person who doubled cannot double again until the other player decides to offer a double. If that is accepted then the doubling cube goes up to show four, and so on all the way up 64. So with our original stake of a dollar, the game could have $64 riding on it.

Do note that it is entirely up to you how you choose to fix stakes at the start. A stake can be per point or it could be per game. It can be an intimidating game when the stakes are high, so be careful if you opt to play for money.

Starting the game

To begin, however, both players roll a single die and the one who scores highest gets to start. He uses the value of his die and that of his opponent and moves pieces accordingly.

From then on you play with your own two dice alternately.

The middle game

Rather like chess, this part of the game is about getting your pieces as far advanced as you can and yet making sure that you impede and lay as many obstacles to smooth progress of your opponent's pieces as you can.

You can build up a substantial lead in the middle game, but do remember that all your opponent has to do is to get one of your pieces back to the bar and you are significantly incommoded.

Ending the game

The bearing off sounds easy, yet your opponent may have opted to keep two players right there on your number one point. That means that even if you have loaded all of your 15 pieces on points 2, 3, 4, 5 and 6, if you move a piece and leave a blot (a single piece on a point), then on his turn he can land on you and send your piece back to the bar. A hit at this stage of the game is liable to mean that you will lose.

Vary your style

What you do not want to be in backgammon is predictable. Vary your approach and you may catch your opponent off guard.

There are three different ways of playing. Firstly, the **hare**. That is someone who just hares away getting as many pieces as far on as possible. Then there is the **blocker approach**, whereby one aims to position pieces on points to block the way of their opponent. This is a defensive approach as opposed to the hare. Finally there is the **back approach**, whereby the player protects the opponent's home square with the intention of hitting them before they can bear off or while they are bearing off.

A little consideration of dice combination odds however will make one realise that there are risks in all of these ways of play. Much will depend upon the skill of your opponent and how much he or she depends on luck or on judicious use of odds.

Good moves and weak moves

Probably the weakest moves are those where you form blots and weaken your play straight away.

It is not a god idea to try to move single pieces too far at the start, especially if they end up as blots.

A strong policy is to get your isolated two pieces in your opponent's home table out of there as soon as you can. You risk having them sealed in there, which is fine if you want to opt for the high risk back game. If you do, just be aware that you will end up trying to roll low scores on the dice, and you can work that out from your knowledge of dice combinations.

It is not a good idea to have too many pieces on any point. You are restricting your options dramatically.

If you are going to have to leave a blot, aim for it to be as far from the opponent pieces as possible, since if they can reach with a seven or a six, they have a very good chance of hitting you.

Towards the end of the game try and block your home table. You will be able to move on it, but if you have managed to hit your opponent back to the bar elsewhere on the board, then he will not be able to restart very easily.

Two of the most important points to block if you can are your bar point and your 5 point. These are really good tactical positions. The bar point is your 7 point, which is adjacent to the bar. The 5 point is in your own home table.

Chapter 19

Role-Playing Games and War-Gaming

This subject could take up a whole book on its own. It certainly accounts for a considerable proportion of the games industry market. The purpose of this chapter is merely to give a flavour of the subject.

Role-playing games have been around for centuries. Indeed, in the early theatre companies of players would wear masks depicting particular characters or emotions. They would give the audience the clue to the character's part, which would be embellished by the actor's performance. The commonly used symbol of drama is the image of a happy face, to depict humour and a sorrowful one to represent tragedy. They actually go back to the days of ancient Greece and are representations of the two faces of Dionysus, the god of theatre and wine. It was said that he could change his nature as quickly as winking. In addition, they show the all too obvious alternate characteristics of wine, one side being merry and the other melancholic in hangover.

These masks were used throughout the development of theatre and were used throughout Europe in the various mystery plays. In the *Commedia dell'arte* in the Sixteenth Century actors would actually start with the characters and improvise a story, effectively making it up on the spot to suit the whims of the audience.

Parallel with live entertainment, of course, games have always been popular. Charades, apparently originated in Provence and derived from '*charra*' meaning chatter. This was a guessing game, a role-playing game in which players act a part or give an impression to their team who have to guess the thing they act out.

Board games also offered a way of taking on roles. In chess, one of course takes on the role of a king, ruling his country and defending it against what seems to be an equally armed and equally affluent country. A battle is to be fought, the terms of which are determined by how the players choose to muster their attacks and defences.

Backgammon, as we have seen is also a game of strategy yet unlike orthodox chess, it permits the entrance of the element of luck through the use of dice. In that game too, as indeed, with all board games you identify with you own pieces and in effect they become an extension of yourself.

Yet, what of creativity! Well you can be creative in the way that you play, but that is creative only in one respect. If you identify with the queen in chess then one queen is pretty much like any other. You have the ability to move in a number of ways but you don't exactly assume any particular character.

This is one of the things missing in so many games and which almost certainly led to the development in the 1970s of role-playing games and which saw the rise of the phenomenon that was to become war-gaming.

The games people play

The 1970s seemed to be a suitable time for the development of various types of role-playing games. The Sixties had gone and with them went flower power, beads, and psychodelia. Yet it left a smouldering desire for fantasy; not the passing clouds type of fantasy but the Lord of the Rings world of demons, orcs, dark wizards and deep, dark places. There was a desire for something a little darker and a bit more abrasive. In the Seventies we had punk culture and in the Eighties it progressed into the positively gothic.

That is not to say that the whole of society was intrigued by the tattoos, chains and metal of punk era, or the black retro clothing and vampire fascination of gothic culture. It is simply that each decade seems to throw up a particular type of counter-culture. The games that people play may reflect that.

The time was right for the invention of Dungeons and Dragons.

HG Wells starts it all off

Before leaping into the world of war-gaming, however, we should look at perhaps the biggest single influence on role-playing games. This was HG Wells, the great writer who gave us such classics as *The War of the Worlds* and *The Invisible Man*. In 1913 he published a book entitled *Little wars: A Game for boys from Twelve Years to One Hundred and Fifty and for that More Intelligent Sort of Girl Who Likes Games and Books*. You may cringe at the title, but the fact is that it is regarded as the blueprint for all the war-gaming that followed.

Wells was an ardent pacifist and in this book he set down the rules for a game of war that he hoped would offer people an outlet for their real aggressive instincts. He advocated using a great sandpit, toy soldiers and toy cannon that could knock down soldiers. It was all to be done according to the rules.

The first cardboard war-game

In 1953 Charles Roberts published the first paper and cardboard war-game, which was called Tactics. It consisted of a board and counters, depicting two post-World War II powers. From then until 1964 his company produced numerous board war-games.

Chainmail

In 1971 a medieval miniature war-game called Chainmail was produced. This consisted of the use of dice to enact battles with miniature figurines. Very specific rules were included so that jousts, melees, hand-to-hand fighting and cavalry charges could be performed. It included a fantasy element and seems to have been the first game to do so.

Dungeons and Dragons

In 1974 this game was designed by Gary Gygax and Dave Arneson and published by Tactical Studies Rules, Inc. Within a short period of time it developed cult status. It is now published by Wizards of the Coast, a subsidiary of Hasbro.

In this game each player is given a character who embarks on an adventure within a mythical landscape. It was ideally suited to a generation that was brought up on the Swords and Fantasy brand of science fiction.

A Dungeon Master acts as the referee and story-teller. He will have access to a Dungeon Master's guide book.

The different characters form a party and they interact with the inhabitants of the mythical setting in order to solve problems, fight battles and gather knowledge and wisdom.

Star Wars and beyond

With successive science fiction movies the number of games has exploded. The sort of games played has also changed with the growing technology. There are still many players of paper and counter war-games, and many miniaturist war-gamers who play with figurines, but now there is inevitably a growing number of computer gamers.

There are advantages and disadvantages in all of them and if you are attracted to this type of game then you have to see which medium suits you best. Computer games will give you an incredible backdrop to play against, but it can be a solitary activity. On the other hand the more old-fashioned paper and counter and miniaturists games are more likely to be social events and affairs and there will be more interaction.

The dice that you use

Having played some of these games, I have to express a preference for the non-computer style of games. Also, being a dice fan I rather like the fact that in some of these games you get to use some of the less used dice that we discussed back in Chapter 2 From Knucklebones to Cyber-dice.

Icosahedron – this is the commonest die used. It has 20 sides and is designated as d20. The faces are equilateral triangles and opposite faces will add up to 21.

Hexahedron or **Cube** – this is the next commonest. It is the standard six-sided die designated as d6. It is used to determine characteristics when you are building a character. Such attributes include dexterity, wisdom, strength and constitution. It is also used to determine various weapon roles.

Dodecahedron – the least used die. It has 12 regular pentagon faces and is designated as d12

Pentagonal trapezohedron – is commonly used. It has 10 kite-shaped faces and is designated as d10. It is usually numbered from 0 to 9, rather than 1 to 10. It is used for deciding the roles of certain weapons.

The **Tetrahedron** – d4, **Octohedron** – d8 and **Zocchihedron** – d100 are all also used.

Now if you want to follow up on this the best thing is to do a little exploration. Perhaps contact a role-playing club or society and go along and see how you like it. You may find that it opens up a whole new world for you.

Have fun!

After-Dice

One last trick

And that is it, a brief journey through the world of dice and dice games. I hope that through these pages you may have found some things of interest and perhaps had a go at one or two of the games that you can play with dice.

I leave you with one last little dice trick that I held back from the chapter on Dice Magic. It is a neat little effect with three dice.

Effect

A spectator rolls three dice. You ask them to do a few simple pieces of arithmetic without showing you the dice. You instantly reveal the numbers they rolled.

Method

You may need to give them a pad and pencil. Ask them to:

- multiply the number on the first die by 2
- add 5 to this total
- multiply this total by 5
- add the number of the second die to this total
- multiply by 10
- add the third die number to this total
- subtract 125 from this total

Presentation

Simply ask them to roll the three dice, then ask them to do these simple calculations. Ask them their total. You then simply subtract 125 from that total and you get a three digit number. Each number will represent one number of the dice they rolled.

Abracadabra!

Dice Glossary

ace – the number one

advantage – the house's (casino's) edge

any craps – a bet in craps that the next roll will be a 2, 3 or 12

any seven – a bet in craps that the next roll will be any combination that makes seven

backgammon – a win in backgammon in which your opponent has a piece in your home table or one piece still on the bar

backline – the Do Not Pass on a craps table

bar – the division between the inner and outer tables in backgammon

bar point – the 7 point adjacent to the bar in backgammon. Strategically a strong point to block.

bevel dice – crooked dice with the edges of one face slightly curved so that they will roll off that face and land on a neighbouring face

blanket roll – a controlled shot with a soft surface such as a carpet or a blanket. Preset dice are held in position then gently rolled so that the end faces of the dice are taken out of the action

block – a point in backgammon with two of a player's pieces on it. An opponent may not land on this point

blot – a point occupied by one piece in backgammon

bones – the dice

bowl – the container for keeping fresh dice

boxcars – in the game of craps this is a double 6

box man – the craps table supervisor

box numbers – the numbers 4, 5, 6, 8, 9 and 10, which are marked inside boxes on a craps table

box up – change of dice

brick – a crooked die made by shaving one face slightly so that the die is like a short brick. Also called a flat

cackle – a false rattle of the dice. The dice are held in such a way that when the hand is moved up and down the dice knock into one another, or cackle. It simulates a rattle

cackle hold – the means of holding two dice to produce a cackle. Also known as the Lock grip

capped dice – crooked dice that have been shaved down and the face capped with another material that will be more elastic than the other faces, so that it will bounce off that face

caster – the thrower in the game of Hazard

chance point – second throw in the game of Hazard

come out roll – the first roll in a game that sets the point (see the game of craps)

crab – a losing throw (a 2 or 3) once the main point has been established in the game of Hazard

deuce – the number 2

dodecahedron – 12 sided die

double deuce – crooked mis-spotted die which has two 2s and no fives

double pitch – when dice have been set and thrown, and one die rotates two or more faces from the set up. The dice have not been controlled

doublet – a double rolled in backgammon

doubling cube – a die with the numbers 2, 4, 8, 16, 32 and 64 instead of pips, which is used to double the stakes in backgammon

five point – the 5 point in the player's home table in backgammon. Strategically a strong point to block

flat – a crooked die made by shaving one face slightly so that the die is like a short brick. Also called a brick

floater – a crooked die which has had a small segment removed so that there is a hollow chamber under one face.

gammon – a win at backgammon in which your opponent has not managed to bear off any pieces

high roll – highest roll on a die to start a game

hit – when a blot is landed on in backgammon, sending a piece to the bar

icosohedron – 20-sided die

level dice – fair, honest dice

lock grip – a means of holding two dice in order to do a false rattle or a cackle

main point – the opening throw in the game of Hazard, which must be between 5 and 9 inclusive

mark – dice swindler's name for a stooge or a sucker, someone to be marked out and swindled.

midnight – a bet that the next roll will be a 12

natural – a 7 or 11 thrown on the come out roll in the game of Craps

nick – a winning throw by the caster in the game of Hazard

octahedron – 8-sided die

one roll bet – a bet that is determined by the next roll

outside numbers – 4, 5, 9, 10

pad roll – another name for a blanket roll

pass – a roll of the point or a natural

passers – crooked dice that are made to favour passes

pit – an area in a casino where the craps tables are found

pit man – the craps tables supervisor

point – one of the triangular shapes on the backgammon board
Also, a number established by the come out roll, but not craps (2, 3 or 12) or a natural (7 or 11), in the game of Craps. That means, either 4, 5, 6, 8, 9, or 10

pentagonal trapezohedron – 10-sided die

percentage dice – fair, honest dice

saw-edged dice – crooked dice with notches on an edge so that they will grip

setter – the person not throwing in the game of Hazard

six-one flat – the commonest brick type of crooked die

shooter – the person throwing at craps

soft roll – another name for a blanket roll

square dice – fair, honest dice

stake – the bet

straight dice – fair, honest dice

tappers – crooked dice with a cylindrical chamber containing mercury. When the mercury is in the middle of the die it throws fair, but when tapped it throws like a loaded die

tetrahedron – 4-sided die

wrong better – in craps someone who bets to lose

Zocchihedron – 100 sided die

Select Bibliography

Finkel, Irving, *Games: Discover and Play 5 Famous Ancient Games,* The British Museum Press, 2009

Jacobs, Gil, *Best of the World's Best Dice Games,* John N Hansen Co, Inc, 1998

Jones, J Philip, *Gambling Yesterday and Today – a complete history,* David and Charles, 1973

Reade, Julian, *Mesopotamia,* The British Museum Press, 1991

Scarne, John, *Scarne on Dice, 8th revised edition,* Wilshire Book Co, 1974

Scarne, John, *Scarne's New Complete Guide to Gambling,* Simon & Schuster, 1974